I0764875

Mastering Girlhood To Womanhood

BOOK 3

LESSONS 14-17

MASTERING GIRLHOOD TO WOMANHOOD
BOOK 3
LESSONS 14-17

Juanita B. Tischendorf

Copyright Page

THIS IS A J. TISCHENDORF BOOK
PUBLISHED BY J TISCHENDORF SERVICES

www.lulu.com

Library of Congress Cataloging in-Publication Data

Tischendorf, Juanita, [date]

MASTERING GIRLHOOD TO WOMANHOOD LESSONS 14-17 / Juanita Tischendorf – 1st ed.

p. cm.

Step by Step Instructional manual for teen girls

Published in the United States of America

ISBN: 978-1-928613-49-7 (Hardcover)
ISBN: 978-1-928613-47-3 (Paperback)
ISBN: 978-1-928613-46-6 (E-Book)

Dedication

This book is dedicated to those teenage girls who want to be the best they can be. MASTERING GIRLHOOD TO WOMANHOOD is a class of instructions that has equal doses of euphoria and agony, and like every part of life, it takes willpower along with dedication to face the journey.

This is the beginning of a four-book presentation of working toward all the aspects that make you who you are. Each book covers a segment of your development until you reach the end. At that point you will know yourself better than you ever thought possible. From your outward appearance, your inward feelings, and your ability to make it in this world.

If this is what you hope for, these books will get you there.

Epigraph

"Stanford Encyclopedia of Philosophy"

The nature of beauty is one of the most enduring and controversial themes in Western philosophy, and is—with the nature of art—one of the two fundamental issues in philosophical aesthetics. Beauty has traditionally been counted among the ultimate values, with goodness, truth, and justice.

Preface

Have you ever felt pulled or twisted from the path you had chosen; as if forces beyond control were at the wheel and you were merely a passenger? If not, you are a lucky person and if so, don't think for a minute you are the only one who has felt as though the oars were being wield by others.

It appears all the important parts of life are controlled and we are merely pawns playing a role. One attempt to make sense of it all is to think that no matter how determined you are to follow the callings of your heart or aim to force yourself to do what is right, it is not your choice that guides you to the outcome. No, it is something called 'destiny' that sits in the driver's seat.

The story I am about to tell you will make a believer out of you or at least have you wondering if it could have been. Because one thing is sure, destiny can lead you into situations that are not as they seem to be.

CONTENTS

INTRODUCTION

Here you are in MASTERING GIRLHOOD TO WOMANHOOD Book 3. In Book 2 you learned the following:

SEND IN THE CLOWNS? : Make-up isn't about rules, it's about options, and there are times when you wish to tone down your strongest features, then later emphasize them. After all, if you want to look great, you certainly need to feel it. Makeup is the art of optical illusion and that takes practice. It all counts here. You need to start with a really clean slate and then work upwards without turning yourself into a clown.

TAMING THE MANE: This is your "crowning" glory. Hair care is the process of improving the appearance by cleansing, conditioning, coloring, or styling. Modern hair care is a blend of science and marketing with hundreds of companies offering thousands of products to solve every possible hair care. Bad hair care tactics, or not taking care of your hair can lead to breakage, fly away, frizziest, split ends, dull hair, and early hair loss. When it comes to hair care, there are a few basic rules that everyone should consider adopting for the long-term health of their strands.

FEATURING THE EXTREMETIES: Lovely hands require pampering to become soft and supple. Not only are first impressions drawn on the skin, but also the nails. Keeping your nails well manicured will improve first impressions. Even your feet which are usually encased in shoes tell a lot about a person . Sore or uncared for feet can lead to medical problems. Most of us do not dry them carefully, especially between the toes where more bacteria collect than anywhere else on your skin.

In order to keep your hands and feet looking fresh, you have to take care of them at home. If you've got extremely dry skin on your hands or your feet, you've probably got a closet full of lotions that haven't done the trick. Whether it's your hands or your feet (or both!) causing you problems, you need to know what works for you.

LESSON 14
WATCHING THOSE CARBS

Stop fooling yourself! At any age you can have unsightly bulges that camouflage the "natural" shape of your body. You are never too young or too old to start learning how to keep or get your body in the shape it was meant to be. Don't be one of the 9.5 Million Americans who go on a diet every year. Or one of the 26 million people who report they are concerned about their waistline. If you fall into this category, then you know how hard it is to find a diet that not only works but also suits your tastes and lifestyle. There is no magical way to rid yourself of excess weight. It takes time and self-discipline to follow a diet plan. Once you have made up your mind to take care of this situation you will be one step further toward reaching your objective.

In thinking about maintaining weight and health, you should remember that how you burn off calories is equally important. If you want to develop and maintain a certain body weight, reducing calorie intake must be accompanied by increasing energy expenditure.

Exercise requires energy, and energy is derived from

foodstuffs stored in the body as fats, proteins, and carbohydrates. The nutritional unit of energy is the calorie, defined as the amount of heat required to raise the temperature of one kilogram of water 1 degree. Exercise draws on the food reserves of the body placed in equal amount. This means that if the food intake is balanced to one calorie supplied and one calorie consumed the result will be a thinner body.

Facts About Food

The first things you need to understand are the facts about food. Food provides you with proteins, carbohydrates, fats, vitamins, minerals, and water. Each of these nutrients has an important function that interacts with the others. Enzymes and acids work with these nutrients in your digestive system transforming proteins into amino acids, carbohydrates into sugars, and fats into fatty acids and glycerol. In the revised form they are absorbed into the bloodstream. Let's take a closer look at the foods you eat and what they provide. While doing this you will also learn how you should change or improve the way you are eating.

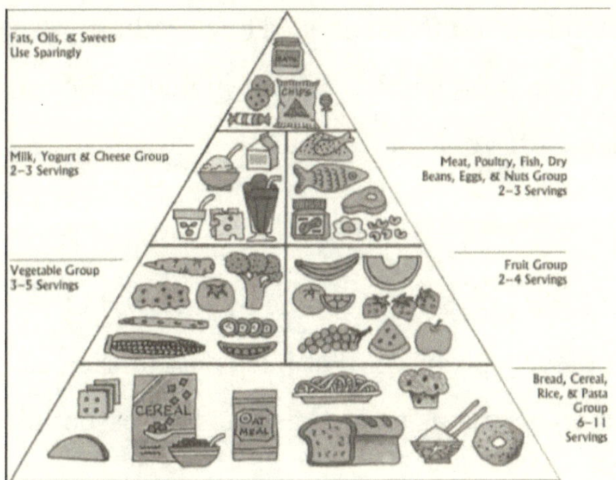

Figure 1: USDA Food Pyramid

Protein

Protein repairs and maintains muscle tissue and cells, supplying energy when carbohydrates and fat reserves are exhausted. Proteins are made up of amino acids. Your muscles, tissues, skin, bone, eyes are all built of protein and kept up and restored by protein.

Your protein rich foods are meats, poultry, fish, eggs, cheese, and many others.

Carbohydrates

Carbohydrates are the chief source of energy. Starch represents the main component of carbohydrates which is turned into glucose in the body and provides energy for the brain, the nervous system, and the muscles.

These are the starches and the sugars. They produce energy, but they also produce fat. By cutting down on them you can slice off your fat.

Fat

Fat is the second most important source of energy, but also a potential dietary problem. Fat insulates, lubricates, protects your internal organs as well as provides essential fatty acids.

With all you've heard about fat, you may believe it's a good idea to try to eliminate it from your diet. You need to cut down on fat, but the truth is you need some fat. On the average, Americans eat 38 percent of their daily intake in the form of fat. Health and nutrition experts say people over the age of twenty should reduce fat to an average of 30 percent.

Limiting the total amount of fat, you eat should include cutting back on how much saturated fat you intake. All fat is made up of saturated, mono-unsaturated, and poly-unsaturated.

What does this mean? Saturated fat has been linked to high blood cholesterol levels and it should be reduced to no more than 10 percent of your daily calories.

Meats, eggs, and dairy products contain the greatest amounts of saturated fats. As long as total fat intake is within the suggested range of not more than 30 percent, substituting poly-unsaturated or mono-unsaturated fats such as olive, peanut, corn, soybean, and safflower oils for saturated fats may help lower blood cholesterol.

Butter, oils, and the fat found in animal and vegetable foods are a vital form of energy. Since these fatty foods contain twice the caloric content of carbohydrates, they should be avoided as much as possible. As a guideline, consider the following levels.

DAILY RECOMMENDED LEVELS		
Calories	Fat (Gms)	Saturated Fat(Gms)
1200	40	13
1500	50	17
1800	60	20
2100	70	23
2400	80	27
2700	90	30
3000	100	33

Cholesterol

To reduce dietary fat in order to lower blood cholesterol, you need to know what cholesterol is. Food such as meat and milk, or animal foods are the source of your cholesterol intake and there are two types of cholesterol:

Low density lipoprotein (LDL) is usually referred to as

bad cholesterol. It is thought to be the culprit in heart disease and contains most of the cholesterol found in the blood. It is also associated with making cholesterol available for cell structures, hormones, and nerve coverings. It is the cholesterol that leaves deposits on artery walls.

High-density lipoprotein (HDL) is usually referred to as good cholesterol. It seems to help remove cholesterol from body tissues and blood, so it can be recycled and used again. The National Heart, Lung and Blood Institute's recommended levels are on the following chart.

HDL Cholesterol	
Under 35 mg/dl	Low
Under 130 mg/dl	Desirable
LDL Cholesterol	
Under 130 mg/dl	Desirable
130 - 159 mg/dl	Borderline-High
160 mg/dl or over	High

Fiber

Fiber, a form of carbohydrate is very important for people who want to lose weight since it decreases the number of calories you absorb from your food.

Fiber is the components of plant foods that are not broken down in the human digestive tract or absorbed into the blood steam. Fiber is a complex carbohydrate and a food you are encouraged to eat more of as you eat less fat, sugar, and cholesterol. Fiber contributes virtually no calories to the diet. You find fiber in whole-grain cereals, breads and many vegetables and fruits.

Eating fiber will help you feel full and satisfied after a meal. It comes in two types: Soluble and Insoluble.

Soluble fiber has been shown to have important effects in digestive and absorptive processes and may help control blood sugar levels. It may also help lower blood cholesterol.

Insoluble fiber draws more water into the intestinal tract and helps keep it there.

A healthy intake of both insoluble and soluble fiber is recommended, or 20 to 40 grams of dietary fiber per day.

Bran fiber is the coarse, outer layer of the whole-grain kernel. Bran contains some starch, protein, a very small amount of fat, iron, and zinc. Depending on the grain source, bran will have different amounts of soluble and insoluble fiber.

The following chart will help you in identifying fibers

and the number of grams consumed. The chart is a listing of the soluble and insoluble fiber amounts from different food sources.

SOLUBLE & INSOLUBLE FIBER				
		TOTALFIBER (gms)	Amount of Fiber (gms)	
FOOD ITEM	SERVING		SOLUBLE	INSOLUBLE
Apple	1 small	2.8	1.0	1.8
Broccoli	1/2 cup	2.8	1.3	1.5
Carrots	1/2 cup	3.2	1.5	1.7
Cheerios	1 1/4 cup	2.0	1.0	1.0
Corn	1/2 cup	1.9	0.2	1.7
Cornflakes	1 cup	0.5	0.1	0.4
Kidney beans	3/4 cup	9.3	2.3	7.0
Oat Bran	1/3 cup	4.0	2.0	2.0
Oatmeal	3/4 cup	2.5	1.2	1.3
Orange	1 medium	1.9	1.1	0.8

Vitamins

Vitamins are distinct from carbohydrates, fats, and proteins in function as well as in the quantities in which you require them. Vitamins are catalysts for the biochemical reactions that take place in the body. Your body cannot manufacture all the vitamins it requires so therefore you must eat foods that supply these vitamins. Vitamins help control most body processes and are important for vision and maintaining healthy tissues. They aid your nerve activity and even help in releasing energy from the foods you eat. Vitamins are organic substances that usually are separated into water-soluble (B Vitamins and Vitamin C) and fat-soluble (Vitamins A,

D, E, K) groups. From .00002 to .005 percent of your diet should include vitamins for normal health and growth. If a vitamin is absent from the diet or is not properly absorbed by an organism, a specific deficiency disease may develop.

Water soluble which are not retained by the body and must be replenished daily. The water soluble include Thiamin (B_1), Riboflavin (B_2), Niacin (B_3), B_6, B_{12}, Biotin, Folic Acid, Pantothenic Acid and Vitamin C. Water-soluble vitamins usually are excreted in the urine of man. If intake begins to exceed minimal requirements, excess vitamins are stored in the tissue. As the tissues become saturated, the rate of excretion increases sharply. This knowledge is valuable in establishing the nutritional status of an individual with respect to the vitamins. Water soluble vitamins generally are not considered toxic if taken in excessive amounts. Water soluble vitamins are an important molecule in controlling the interconversion (n a process in which two things are each converted into the other, often as the result of chemical or physical activity) of fats, proteins and carbohydrates and their conversion into metabolic energy.

Fat soluble are stored in the fatty tissue of the body and can build up with time. The fat soluble includes Vitamins

A, D, E and K. The Vitamin A group has at least one known function. In the retina of the eye, retinal is combined with a protein called opsin. The complex molecules formed because of this combination and known as rhodopsin are involved in dark vision. Vitamin D is required for growth. Vitamin E is necessary for normal human functions such as reproduction, and the elimination of abnormalities in the central nervous system. Vitamin K is necessary for the proper clotting of blood. Fat-soluble vitamins are transported primarily by lymph from the intestines to the circulating blood. Larger quantities of fat-soluble vitamins than water-soluble can be stored in the body. Vitamins A, D and K are stored chiefly in the liver, with smaller amounts stored in other soft body tissues. Most of the stored Vitamin E is found in body fat or in the uterus of females and testis of males.

Think of vitamins as glamour foods. Vitamin A brings sparkle to your eyes and a glow to your skin. It is found in yellow and green vegetables, fresh fruit, liver, and milk. Vitamin B should be called happiness vitamin because whenever the diet is lacking it, humans tend to become depressed. Vitamin B is found in calf or lamb liver, brains, sweetbreads, and kidneys. Wheat germ, brewer's yeast, fresh or powdered milk are also sources to consider for absent-minded or moody feelings.

Vitamin C keeps up the maintenance of a substance called collagen that binds the body cells into solid tissue. A lack of collagen is evident in easy bruising or bleeding gums. Vitamin C is found in citrus fruits and other fruits as well as many of the yellow vegetables. Vitamin D keeps your bones strong and straight.

Vitamin D is hard to find in ordinary foods as it is induced by direct sunshine and ultraviolet light on exposed skin surfaces. You find Vitamin D in eggs, fish oils, blue fin tuna which is more potent with Vitamin D than even cod liver oil.

You may be asking yourself if you should take vitamin pills rather than trying to eat well. Getting your vitamins in the form of pills is okay, but you should be aware that tests conducted on multivitamins and mineral products showed that many kinds of pills pass through the body untouched. The U.S. Food and Drug Administration regards supplements as foods, not drugs, which means the agency sets few rules for how the pills must be formulated or manufactured. There is no law that requires a vitamin producer to prove that a tablet or capsule will break up into small pieces, as it should after it has been swallowed or dissolved in fluids so that the body can absorb the active ingredients. The only requirement is that the supplement contains the actual amounts that it claims on the label. As a guide, the following brands of vitamins do breakdown once ingested: CVS, Rite Aid, Your Life, Shaklee, Centrum,

GNC Solotron and One-A-Day. Doctors agree that by reading the labels on these vitamins you can get an idea of what to look for on the label of the vitamins you select. Doctors recommend you consult your doctor and ask his advice about the vitamins you are taking. But you should try and eat the foods that supply the vitamins and minerals your system requires.

Minerals

Minerals are needed by your body as a building block for tissue, strong bones, strong teeth, and regulators of metabolic processes. Water is required for every bodily function from digestion, to regulating your temperature, to transporting nutrients, to removing body wastes. Minerals are inorganic, meaning they do not contain the element carbon. The dietary minerals are calcium, iron, potassium, sodium, phosphorus, magnesium, and zinc.

Minerals are also needed by your body. There are sixteen

essential minerals found widely in every day foods. There are three that are hard to find in foods--Calcium, Iron, and Iodine. Take special care to make sure your diet is rich in these three minerals.

Calcium exists in all dairy products such as milk, skim milk, powdered milk, buttermilk, and cheese as well as yogurt. Iodine exists in sea foods such as fish, shellfish, kelp, sea lettuce and sea greens.

Calcium

Calcium is vital for healthy bones and teeth. It also is important in the normal functioning of muscles and nerves, blood clotting and hormonal system functions.

Dairy products, leafy green vegetables, tortillas, tofu, and the soft bones of fish are sources of calcium. The recommended daily allowance for calcium is 800 milligrams per day for people twenty-five years and older and 1200 milligrams for those below twenty-five.

For those with lactose intolerance for dairy foods, there is lactose free milk and medication to alleviate the problem. Doctors state that if you find milk and dairy products upset your stomach, consult your doctor, and concentrate on eating the other foods that can provide you with the calcium you need.

The following chart shows the calcium content of food. Using this chart, you can begin to learn how to meet the daily calcium requirements. The serving sizes play an important role. So, in choosing foods rich in calcium, be sure to eat the amounts specified or you won't meet the calcium level that is listed.

FOOD	SERVING SIZE	CALCIUM (mgs)
Beans	1 cup	90
Broccoli	1/2 cup	90
American Cheese	1 oz.	174
Cottage Cheese	1/2 cup	77
Cheddar Cheese	1 oz.	204
Mozzarella Cheese	1 oz.	207
Swiss Cheese	1 oz.	272
Ice Cream	1/2 cup	88
Ice Milk	1/2 cup	88
Buttermilk	1 cup	285
Whole Milk	1 cup	291
1% Milk	1 cup	300
2% Milk	1 cup	297
Skim Milk	1 cup	302
Chocolate pudding	1/2 cup	133
Salmon	3 oz.	167
Sardines	3 oz	371
Spinach	1/2 cup	122
Tofu	4 oz.	108
Low-Fat Fruited Yogurt	1 cup	345
Low-Fat Plain Yogurt	1 cup	415

In eating for health and beauty you should:

- Substitute low-fat foods for those high fat content foods
- Cut down on meat by eating low on the food chain
- Avoid salt and salty foods
- Cut down on sugar
- Place great emphasis on whole grains
- Beware of alcohol.
- Eat raw unsalted nuts and sesame seeds
- Eat sprouted seeds such as soybeans
- Eat fresh raw wheat bran and wheat germ
- Eat yogurt and kefir
- Eat plenty of fresh fruits and vegetables

If you want to eat for health and lose weight you should understand that there is only one way to do it. You must decrease the amount of food you eat and increase the amount of exercise you get. That is all there is to it. Starving, crash diets or subsisting on small amounts of food is not the way to lose weight. These methods will see the weight return once you resume your normal eating patterns.

Think of food as what it was meant to be. Fuel for your Body.

Calories

You hear a great deal about calories and yet only one woman in ten knows what a calorie really is, and one in a thousand knows how many calories she consumes in a day. A Calorie is simply a unit of measuring heat and the energy value of food. Calories are not food. There are some foods that are high in caloric value which makes it harder to burn them up entirely in energy. When a calorie is not burned up it turns into body fat. Therefore, calorie counting is so very important.

How many calories do you consume each day? Would you say 1000, 2000, 3000, 4000 or more? This is not an area to guess at, you need to know the exact number of calories you are eating on an average day. You also need to know just what the foods you are now consuming contain. You will do this by filling out the forms that follow and list the information requested. Don't change your normal eating habits as you need an accurate recording to help you make decisions on how you will be able to lose, gain, or retain your present weight.

Most of the information will be provided on the labels of the food you purchase, but you need a little more information before you proceed.

How To Read Food Labels

To help you in accurately recording your information, the following is a sample of a food product label. The labels on food recently underwent changes that benefit the consumer by making it more apparent exactly what you are getting from the product. Before then, the labels were not as easy to decipher.

Following is a sample of the information that is now required to appear on labels. You should look this over and review the information that follows. This will help you understand the breakdown and what you should be looking for in the products you buy.

LABEL INFORMATION	
NUTRITIONAL INFORMATION PER SERVING	
Serving Size	1 oz.
Servings per container	4
Calories	160
Protein (grams)	12
Carbohydrates (grams)	12
Fat (grams)	11
Sodium (milligrams)	10
Cholesterol (milligrams)	0

The Nutrition Facts label appears on the side or back panel of almost all packaged foods in the grocery store. Use them to keep track of the nutritional content, including calories and fat, of every food product you buy. Below are sample labels for packages of bacon, bagels and bananas.

BACON

Nutrition Facts	
Serving Size 2 slices (13g)	
Servings Per Container 10	
Amount Per Serving	
Calories 70	Calories from Fat 60
	%Daily Value*
Total Fat 6g	10 %
Saturated Fat 2.5g	11 %
Cholesterol 10mg	4 %
Sodium 210mg	9 %
Total Carbohydrate 0g	0 %
Dietary Fiber 0g	0 %
Sugars 0g	
Protein 4g	
Vitamin A 0% •	Vitamin C 0%
Calcium 0% •	Iron 0%
* Percent Daily Values are based on a 2,000 calorie diet.	

LOW=5% or less HIGH=20% or more

BAGEL

Nutrition Facts	
Serving Size 1 bagel (71g)	
Servings Per Container 5	
Amount Per Serving	
Calories 200	Calories from Fat 10
	%Daily Value*
Total Fat 1g	2 %
Saturated Fat 0g	0 %
Cholesterol 0mg	0 %
Sodium 380mg	16 %
Total Carbohydrate 38g	13 %
Dietary Fiber 2g	7 %
Sugars 2g	
Protein 7g	
Vitamin A 0% •	Vitamin C 0%
Calcium 6% •	Iron 15%
* Percent Daily Values are based on a 2,000 calorie diet.	

LOW=5% or less HIGH=20% or more

BANANA

Nutrition Facts	
Serving Size 1 banana (118g)	
Servings Per Container 6	
Amount Per Serving	
Calories 110	Calories from Fat 5
	%Daily Value*
Total Fat 0.5g	1 %
Saturated Fat 0g	0 %
Cholesterol 0mg	0 %
Sodium 0mg	0 %
Total Carbohydrate 28g	9 %
Dietary Fiber 3g	11 %
Sugars 18g	
Protein 1g	
Vitamin A 0% •	Vitamin C 20%
Calcium 0% •	Iron 2%
* Percent Daily Values are based on a 2,000 calorie diet.	

LOW=5% or less HIGH=20% or more

Sample Food Labels

To calculate the percentage of calories from fat in any food, multiply the number of grams of fat per serving by 9. Divide the fat calories by the total calories, and then multiply this figure by 100 to find the percent. Look at the example of the label information. In using this formula, the calculation would look like this:

11 x 9=99 99 ÷ 160 = 0.62 0.62 x 100 = 62% calories from fat

The American Heart Association recommends that approximately 55% of the day's calories come from carbohydrates. To determine carbohydrate calories, multiply the grams of carbohydrates per serving by 4 then follow the procedure above for fat by dividing your answer by the total calories and multiplying by 100 to get the percentage. Look at the example of the label information. In using this formula, the calculation would look like this:

12 x 4 = 48   48 ÷ 160 = 0.30   0.30 x 100 = 30% calories from carbohydrates

You can use the same method to determine the percent of protein calories. Using the food tables at the end of this chapter or go out and purchase a food calorie counter; you should begin to keep track your calorie intake for a week to get a handle on how many calories you enjoy consuming each day.

To make this exercise dual-purpose, once you have recorded your food intake and noted the calorie content, figure out if you are getting enough calcium, fiber, and how much of your intake is from fat, carbohydrates, and protein. All of this is available on the packaging label, so mark it down.

Take the time to get your cholesterol level read and record the findings, then fill in the charts accurately so you will have the information needed to begin changing your eating habits.

FOOD INTAKE CHART #1					
		TOTALS			
		Calories	FAT (gm)	Calcium	Fiber (gm)
Breakfast					
Lunch					
Dinner					
Snacks					

FOOD INTAKE CHART #2					
		TOTALS			
		Calories	FAT (gm)	Calcium	Fiber (gm)
Breakfast					
Lunch					
Dinner					
Snacks					

FOOD INTAKE CHART #3					
		TOTALS			
		Calories	FAT (gm)	Calcium	Fiber (gm)
Breakfast					
Lunch					
Dinner					
Snacks					

FOOD INTAKE CHART #4					
		TOTALS			
		Calories	FAT (gm)	Calcium	Fiber (gm)
Breakfast					
Lunch					
Dinner					
Snacks					

FOOD INTAKE CHART #5					
		TOTALS			
		Calories	FAT (gm)	Calcium	Fiber (gm)
Breakfast					
Lunch					
Dinner					
Snacks					

FOOD INTAKE CHART #6					
		TOTALS			
		Calories	FAT (gm)	Calcium	Fiber (gm)
Breakfast					
Lunch					
Dinner					
Snacks					

FOOD INTAKE CHART #7					
		TOTALS			
		Calories	FAT (gm)	Calcium	Fiber (gm)
Breakfast					
Lunch					
Dinner					
Snacks					

Your Present Eating Habits

You should now have a handle on your eating habits and know what you are consuming. If your present eating habits give you a varied and nutritional diet, it will be safe to cut 500 to 750 calories per day from your present total to lose weight or add up to 1000 calories more to gain weight. If you cut out 500 calories from your normal daily in-take you will lose more than a pound a week easily. A pound doesn't seem like much until you figure that over 10 weeks it represents 10 pounds!

If you are more than 20 pounds overweight and can't live a minute longer with yourself, first think about how long it took you to get that way. If that doesn't help, then maybe to start you should consider a special diet. By this I mean that you should consult a physician for a physical, tell him your intentions and with professional help this may be the safe thing for you to do. But remember: Step one is to see a doctor before going on such a diet.

Now here is what you do if you want to lose weight. Simply cut down on the foods that put the most weight on you. This way you can eat more of other foods. The objective is to cut out 500 to 750 calories a day by decreasing your intake of carbohydrates, oils, and fats, while you increase your intake of proteins and certain vitamins and minerals. Try to stay away from the foods that offer the least body needs and you will lose weight. You should also consider eliminating the gravy on your meats, rice, and potatoes!

Minimum Daily Food Requirements

From all you have read you are probably thinking that you must be a nutrition expert to know how to eat healthfully. Not so. You can learn how to balance your fat, cholesterol, fiber, calcium, and sodium. All it takes is paying attention to what you eat. It's easy if you take it one step at a time. You might approach it by trying first to build a good foundation of understanding the foods you eat and what they contain. The foundation of a well-balanced diet is eating a wide variety of foods. No single food will give you all the nutrients you need. It all is in your attitude of how serious you are about eating right and then taking the steps to change toward a more sensible diet.

To help you begin eating healthy, the following are the minimum daily food requirements set by the United States Department of Agriculture:

Minimum Daily Food Requirements

MILK - 2 or more glasses

VEGETABLES - 2 or more servings, green or yellow

FRUITS - 2 servings, 1 a citrus fruit or tomato

EGGS - 1; at least 3 to 5 a week

MEAT, FISH, POULTRY, CHEESE - 1 or more servings

CEREAL AND BREAD - 2 servings, whole grains or enriched

In trying to lose weight:

- Watch the candy, canapés, sodas, sandwiches, cream cheeses.
- Cultivate a taste for Melba toast or Swedish rye bread.
- Go heavy on leafy green vegetables.
- Become a tomato juice fan. Try various unsweetened fruit juices.
- Become a fancier of fruit.
- Eat yogurt. Use milk rather than cream; especially skimmed milk.
- Spices tend to hold weight so season foods less.
- Trim off fats on meats, broil or bake foods rather than fry them.
- Kiss cream sauces goodbye.
- Use a non-fattening sugar substitute.

Try not to dwell on foods you can't have and consider the quantities of food that you can have in the low-calorie group. As you eat these low-calorie foods, tell yourself how much you will enjoy the compliments that will be coming your way as you slim down and retain that figure for the rest of your life. The following are examples of high caloric foods that you should start now to consider as ***NO-NOS:***

High Caloric Foods

MALTED MILK	400
COFFEE CAKE	100
CHOCOLATE CREAM	175
TARTAR SAUCE	100
GRAVIES	100
CHOCOLATE SUNDAE	350
CREAM PUFF	175
PIES	400

The above calorie counts are based on average consumption, not above average consumption. Stay away from these and it won't matter the quantity included in the average portions.

Remember you will still need to exercise. The advantages of a good exercise program are covered in the section that follows. Exercise will help you burn up the calories you intake. It is exercise that works to burn calories, not a massage.

A massage will not take off pounds or put them on, it

simply tones the muscles and helps to firm flesh that might end up hanging in folds if you try a quick weight loss diet. Massages have a notable function since they tend to improve circulation. Having a massage once a week can do wonders along with proper diet and exercise.

Using electrical vibrators or rollers for weight reduction lies in the belief that the individual using them does not have to do anything. You may note a change of measurement, but the decrease will return when you stop. If you don't combine diet, a good strenuous (your own exertion) exercise program, and sensible thinking and planning, you will lose in your effort to lose weight and keep it off. And along with this sensible way of losing weight, you should strive to get a full night's sleep.

Gaining Weight

If you need to gain weight, you know that this can also be a problem. To gain weight avoid pastry, cakes, white breads, and fried foods. Do not overload your system with fats. Eat lean meats, broiled, and baked. Eat the dark breads that are richer in vitamins and be certain that you eat your full quota of foods recommended by the YOU Government each day. More nutritious foods will do more for you than the fatty foods. You need foods rich in energy, not just in bulk. You need to rest more and try to decrease your busy schedule. Try sleeping an extra ten minutes longer each morning. Be sure to get at least eight hours sleep each night. Try to get nine when you can.

Another area to consider is worry and tension. This can take the value of a good diet away from you. After finding your ideal weight and increasing your intake by 1000 calories to gain weight, also get yourself a book on the number of calories that can be expected to be burned in exercising activities and/or sports. You may have to add on even more since you still need exercise.

While others say, "What a Problem", in that way they have, never fear, there are those who know that this can be as big a problem as trying to lose weight. You just must remember to do it the right way!

Dieting Tips

Doctors caution that before embarking on any diet you should consult your doctor for his advice. Not any one type of diet is right for everyone and certain medical conditions require very specific diets, such as diabetes. If you are physically healthy, here are some tips that will help you reach your goal once you make up your mind to diet.

- Don't wait until you've gained a lot of weight before you start dieting.
- Try to weigh yourself at least once a week so you will be aware of the weight creeping upon you.
- Try and start a diet as soon as you gain about five pounds.
- Make a small alteration in your daily routine just to prove to yourself that you can change if you set your mind to it.
- Start waking up an hour earlier, or delay dinner by an hour, and use the time to do some exercises. Exercise is very important when you are dieting since it's the best way to reduce body fat, diminish appetite and build well-toned muscle tissue to give you a leaner, firmer figure.
- Don't start out by setting a long term ideal weight goal. Instead decide to diet until you feel comfortable with your weight and like the way you look.
- Be conservative in your short-term goals. The average weight loss for adult women on a diet is two and a half to three pounds per week. It's unrealistic to expect to lose ten pounds every week.
- Before starting a diet, make a list of past dieting efforts and the reasons they failed. Learn from

your mistakes and choose a new regimen that helps you avoid or overcome these problems.

- If you can't seem to get started on a formal diet, try eliminating certain fattening foods on a short-term basis. For instance, cut out chocolate, butter and fiber foods for a week. Once these are under control you'll gain confidence and stick to your weight loss plan.
- It's easiest to start with a plan that prescribes exact menus with little leeway for substitutions. When you first begin a diet, you'll feel more comfortable if you don't have to make decisions about eating.
- If you find there are too many distractions and stresses at home, try a health spa or diet clinic, or stay with a supportive friend for the first few days of a diet. If you can't get away from home, try to avoid some of the everyday stress by hiring a baby sitter, or taking the phone off the hook.
- Be in control of everything you eat. Never put food in your mouth without first thinking. Do I really need this! Am I really all that hungry! A few setbacks are bound to occur so don't consider yourself a failure if you slip. Instead, admit your error, figure out why it happened and write it down, so you can avoid it next time.
- Keep a list of your successes. Make a notation

whenever you lose weight or have the strength to pass up fattening foods. Keep this list handy and check it at moments of weakness for a little extra encouragement. If you do yield to temptation, get right back on schedule. If you break your diet on Saturday, don't wait until Monday to resume.

- Don't eat on the run. Sit down and enjoy your food, chew it slowly and really taste it--and stop eating as soon as you feel full.
- Avoid comparing yourself to others. Concentrate on your own goals, and don't be jealous of another person's progress. Try not to think of dieting as a moral issue in which it's bad to eat and good to deny yourself. Dieting is simply a method to take off pounds. It's not a pitched battle of virtue against vice.
- Don't isolate yourself because you don't want to burden others. It makes dieting harder if you remove yourself from people who care about you. Ask for help and support when you need it but be sure you are the one who takes the responsibility for what, when and where you eat.
- Don't blame all your problems on being overweight on heredity, family eating habits or circumstances beyond your control.
- Don't fantasize that once you are slim you won't

have any troubles. This kind of unrealistic thinking can sabotage a diet. You can't practice complete self-denial forever; it's more effective to learn control. Allow yourself a small portion of a favorite fattening food occasionally, as a reward for sticking to your diet.

- When you know you will be facing temptations, prepare yourself by planning food choices ahead of time.
- Try to keep yourself busy--too much spare time and boredom are leading causes of mindless nibbling.
- Do everything you can to minimize exposure to food. If possible, don't keep fattening foods in the house, and try to spend as little time as you can shopping for food and preparing it.
- Eat four balanced, low-calorie meals a day that add up to the total caloric intake for you to lose weight and never eat after 7:00 pm. Skipping a meal isn't much of an accomplishment if it leads to a binge later.
- Satisfy your sweet tooth with naturally sweet foods. Fruit quells hunger and provides for more nourishment than junk food. Be a creative shopper. Remember that the most filling low-calorie foods are fresh fruits and vegetables.

- Avoid eating in secret. Everyone has favorite foods with high emotional value. Consuming them in public devalues such foods, makes them less important and less satisfying.
- Drink at least eight large glasses of water a day. Space them out. If you eat 4 meals a day, have a glass before and one after each of your meals.
- Have hot liquids before meals to help fill you up. Herbal tea and hot soup are excellent meal starters.
- Experiment with serving techniques that make small portions look larger. Give your appearance special attention while you diet.
- Pamper yourself with a beauty treatment at a salon or some new clothes. Don't deny yourself dinners out but take responsibility for what you eat.
- Allow at least four weeks to adjust to your diet. Even if you have only a few pounds to lose, do it gradually. A successful diet teaches you to control forever your desire for unhealthy foods. It's easier to lose weight at the beginning of a diet because the novelty and encouragement of taking weight off quickly make it exciting for the first few weeks. After that expect to draw more on self-discipline.
- Think up ways to keep yourself motivated.

Stressful events cause some people to overeat. Try at least to maintain your weight until the stress passes and then resume your diet.

Once you achieve your desired weight, work hard at staying there. Maintenance is the hardest part.

You begin to see the "new you" without really seeing you. In other words, don't become so sure of yourself at the end of a successful diet regimen that you refuse to believe the scale warnings or the snug clothes as anything but the truth. Just keep it utmost in your mind how hard it was the first time to get to this point.

The following food tables can help you further in making the choices of foods to include in your diet plan. Consider not only the calories but the fat, protein, carbohydrates and cholesterol content of the foods and you will reap the benefits.

These charts, along with the information in this chapter, will lead you toward a slimmer and healthier you. If you aren't trying to lose weight, you can use these charts to help you select the foods that will give you the benefits you need to have a sound healthy body. Remember, eating right is important whether you want to lose or gain weight and learning how to eat properly will give you a life time of benefits!

PORTION	Calories	Total Fat (Gm)	Sat Fat (Gm)	Protein (Gms)	Carb (Gms)	Choles (Mgs)
POULTRY, SEAFOOD & MEATS (3½ oz.)						
Chicken Breast w/skin	195	8	2	30	0	83
Chicken Breast skinless	164	4	1	31	0	84
Chicken Thigh w/skin	245	15	4	25	0	92
Chicken Thigh skinless	207	11	3	26	0	94
Chicken Liver	156	5	2	24	0	626
Turkey Breast w/skin	197	8	2	29	0	76
Turkey Breast skinless	153	3	1	30	0	68
Turkey Dark Meat w/Skin	221	12	3	27	0	89
Turkey Dark Meat skinless	184	7	2	28	0	87
Turkey Giblets	166	5	2	26	0	415
Turkey ground (Dark)	227	14	4	24	0	68
Turkey ground (White)	153	3	1	30	0	68
Duck w/skin	334	28	10	19	0	83
Duck skinless	189	7	2	29	0	88
FINFISH (3½ oz.)						
Cod	104	*	*	23	0	55
Flounder	116	2	*	24	0	67
Halibut	139	3	*	26	0	41
Mackerel	260	18	4	24	0	74
Redfish	120	2	*	24	0	55
Salmon, sockeye	216	11	2	27	0	87
Sea Bass	123	3	*	23	0	53
Snapper	127	2	*	26	0	47
Swordfish	154	5	1	25	0	50
Trout, rainbow	150	4	*	26	0	72
Tuna white in oil	185	8	n/a	26	0	31
Tuna white in water	135	2	*	26	0	42

Sat=Saturated, Carbs=Carbohydrates,

Choles=Cholesterol, gm=grams, mg=milligrams

* Contains less than 1 gram

PORTION	Calories	Total Fat (Gm)	Sat Fat (Gm)	Protein (Gms)	Carb (Gms)	Choles (Mgs)
SHELLFISH (3½ oz.)						
Clams	147	2	*	25	0	66
Crab, Alaskan King	96	2	*	19	0	53
Lobster	97	*	*	20	0	71
Oysters, raw	68	2	*	7	0	55
Scallops, raw	87	*	*	17	0	33
Shrimp, cooked	98	1	*	21	0	193
BEEF (3½ oz.) [LEAN]						
Flank Steak	205	10	4	27	0	66
Porterhouse	303	22	9	25	0	82
Prime rib	355	29	12	22	0	83
Round Steak	190	7	3	29	0	77
Tenderloin	209	10	4	28	0	83
Ground, extra-lean	254	16	6	25	0	83
Ground, lean	270	18	7	25	0	86
Ground regular	287	21	8	24	0	89
Liver	160	5	2	24	0	386
VEAL (3½ oz.) [LEAN]						
Ground	171	8	3	24	0	102
Loin chop	224	9	3	33	0	124
LAMB (3½ oz.) [LEAN]						
Leg Shank	179	7	2	28	0	86
Loin Chops	214	10	3	30	0	94
Rack Rib	356	30	13	21	0	96
PORK (3½ oz.) [LEAN]						
Bacon	572	49	17	30	0	84
Canadian Bacon	184	8	3	24	0	58
Fresh Ham	219	11	4	29	0	95
Center Loin	314	22	8	27	0	96

Sat=Saturated, Carbs=Carbohydrates,

Choles=Cholesterol, gm=grams, mg=milligrams

* Contains less than 1 gram

PORTION	Calories	Total Fat (Gm)	Sat Fat (Gm)	Protein (Gms)	Carb (Gms)	Choles (Mgs)
PORK (3½ oz.) [LEAN]						
Shoulder	323	25	9	22	0	95
Tenderloin	165	5	2	29	0	92
Ham, boneless, canned	226	15	5	21	0	62
Spareribs	394	30	12	29	0	120
FRUIT						
Apple (1 med)	81	*	*	*	21	670
Apricots, (8 halves)	67	*	*	1	17	0
Avocado (1med)	324	31	5	4	15	0
Banana (1 med)	105	*	*	1	27	0
Cantaloupe (½ cup)	28	*	*	*	7	0
Cherries, sweet (10 large)	49	*	*	*	11	0
Dates, dried (2)	46	*	*	*	12	0
Grapefruit (½))	38	*	*	*	10	0
Grapes, seedless (½ cup)	57	*	*	*	14	0
Orange (1 med)	69	*	*	1	17	0
Peach (1 med)	56	*	*	*	15	0
Pear (1 med)	98	*	*	*	25	0
Pineapple (½ cup)	38	*	*	*	10	0
Plum (1 med)	36	*	*	*	9	0
Prunes, dried (3)	60	*	*	*	16	0
Raisins (2 tbsp.)	54	*	*	*	14	0
Raspberries (½ cup)	30	*	*	*	7	0
Strawberries (½ cup)	23	*	*	*	5	0
Watermelon (½ cup)	26	*	*	*	6	0

Sat=Saturated, Carbs=Carbohydrates,

Choles=Cholesterol, gm=grams, mg=milligrams

* Contains less than 1 gram

PORTION	Calories	Total Fat (Gm)	Sat Fat (Gm)	Protein (Gms)	Carb (Gms)	Choles (Mgs)
VEGETABLES						
Artichokes, Globe (1 med)	53	*	*	3	12	0
Asparagus (½ cup)	23	*	*	2	4	0
Beans, green (½ cup)	22	*	*	1	5	0
Beans, lima, large (½ cup)	108	*	*	7	20	0
Broccoli (½ cup)	23	*	*	2	4	0
Cabbage (½ cup)	8	*	*	*	2	0
Carrots (½ cup)	24	*	*	*	6	0
Corn (½ cup)	89	1	*	3	21	0
Lettuce (½ cup)	5	*	*	*	*	0
Mushrooms (½ cup)	9	*	*	*	2	0
Peas (½ cup)	62	*	*	4	11	0
Pepper, Bell (½ cup)	13	*	*	*	3	0
Potato w/skin (1 med)	220	*	*	5	51	0
Potato skinless (½ cup)	67	*	*	1	16	0
Potato Sweet w/skin(1 med)	117	*	*	2	28	0
Spinach (½ cup)	6	*	*	*	*	0
Squash Summer (½ cup)	18	*	*	*	4	0
Squash Winter (½ cup)	40	*	*	*	9	0
Tomatoes (½ cup)	17	*	*	*	4	0
OILS						
Canola (1 tbsp.)	120	14	*	8	4	0
Coconut (1 tbsp.)	120	14	12	*	*	0
Corn (1 tbsp.)	120	14	2	3	8	0
Cottonseed (1 tbsp.)	120	14	4	2	7	0
Grape seed (1 tbsp.)	120	14	1	2	10	0
Olive (1 tbsp.)	120	14	2	10	1	0
Palm (1 tbsp.)	120	14	7	5	1	0
Palm kernel (1 tbsp.)	120	14	11	2	*	0

Sat=Saturated, Carbs=Carbohydrates,

Choles=Cholesterol, gm=grams, mg=milligrams

* Contains less than 1 gram

PORTION	Calories	Total Fat (Gm)	Sat Fat (Gm)	Protein (Gms)	Carb (Gms)	Choles (Mgs)
OILS						
Peanut (1 tbsp.)	120	14	2	6	4	0
Safflower (1 tbsp.)	120	14	1	2	10	0
Sesame (1 tbsp.)	120	14	2	5	6	0
Soybean (1 tbsp.)	120	14	2	6	5	0
Sunflower (1 tbsp.)	120	14	1	3	9	0
Walnut (1 tbsp.)	120	14	1	3	9	0
BREADS, PASTA, GRAINS, LEGUMES, NUTS						
Bread Rye (1 oz.)	69	*	*	3	15	*
Bread White (1 oz.)	57	*	*	2	14	*
Bread, Whole Wheat (1 oz.)	69	1	*	3	13	*
Crackers, Graham (4square)	109	3	*	2	21	0
Crackers Saltine (10)	123	3	*	3	20	0
Doughnut, Glazed (1)	170	10	2	2	19	11
English Muffin (1)	130	1	*	4	26	n/a
Roll (hot or Frank) (1)	119	2	*	3	21	2
Roll, Hard (1)	156	2	*	5	30	2
Tortilla Corn (1)	67	1	*	2	3	0
Macaroni (½ cup)	99	*	*	3	20	0
Noodles, Egg (½ cup)	106	1	*	4	20	26
Rice, Brown (½ cup)	108	*	*	3	22	0
Rice White (½ cup)	132	*	*	3	29	0
Beans, Black (½ cup)	114	*	*	8	20	0
Beans Pinto (½ cup)	117	*	*	7	22	0
Lentils (½ cup)	115	*	*	9	20	0
Soybeans (½ cup)	149	8	1	14	9	0
Almonds (1 oz.)	167	15	1	6	6	0
Cashews, Salted (1 oz.)	163	14	3	5	8	0
Peanuts Salted (1 oz.)	165	14	2	7	5	0

Sat=Saturated, Carbs=Carbohydrates,

Choles=Cholesterol, gm=grams, mg=milligrams

* Contains less than 1 gram

PORTION	Calories	Total Fat (Gm)	Sat Fat (Gm)	Protein (Gms)	Carb (Gms)	Choles (Mgs)
BREADS, PASTA, GRAINS, LEGUMES, NUTS						
Peanut Butter (1 tbsp.)	95	8	1	5	3	0
Pecans (1 oz.)	189	19	2	2	5	0
Walnuts, English (1 oz.)	182	18	2	4	5	0
OTHER (FATS, DAIRY						
Butter (1 tbsp.)	102	12	7	*	*	31
Lard (1 tbsp.)	116	13	5	*	*	12
Margarine, Corn Oil (1tbsp)	102	11	2	*	*	0
Margarine, Safflower (1tbsp)	1091	11	1	0	0	0
Mayonnaise (1 tbsp.)	99	11	2	*	*	8
Vegetable Shortening(1tbsp)	113	13	3	0	0	0
Egg (1 large)	75	5	2	6	*	213
Egg Yolk (11)	59	5	2	3	*	213
Egg White (1)	17	0	0	4	*	0
Buttermilk (1 cup)	98	2	1	8	12	10
Condensed Milk Sweet(¼ cup)	246	7	4	6	42	26
Evaporated Milk Skim(¼ cup)	50	*	*	5	7	3
Evaporated Milk Whole(¼ cup)	84	5	3	4	6	18
Milk Whole (1 cup)	149	8	5	8	11	34
Milk Low-fat 2% (1 cup)	122	5	3	8	12	20
Milk Skim (1 cup)	86	*	*	8	12	5
Milk Chocolate (1 cup)	208	8	5	*	26	30
Creamer Liquid (1 tbsp.)	20	2	*	*	2	0
Creamer Powder (2 tbsps.)	64	4	4	*	6	0
Half and Half (1 tbsp.)	20	2	1	*	*	6
Sour Cream (1 tbsp.)	31	3	2	1	*	6
Sour Cream Lite (1 tbsp.)	25	2	1	*	1	5
Whipping cream (1 tbsp.)	43	5	3	*	*	17
Whip Cream Can (1 tbsp.)	10	*	*	*	*	3

Sat=Saturated, Carbs=Carbohydrates,

Choles=Cholesterol, gm=grams, mg=milligrams

* Contains less than 1 gram

PORTION	Calories	Total Fat (Gm)	Sat Fat (Gm)	Protein (Gms)	Carb (Gms)	Choles (Mgs)
OTHER (FATS, DAIRY						
Dessert Topping (1 tbsp.)	9	*	*	*	*	*
Yogurt Plain (8 oz.)	138	7	5	8	11	29
Yogurt Plain Low-fat (8 oz.)	143	4	2	12	16	14
Yogurt Low-fat w/Fruit (8 oz.)	231	2	2	10	43	9
Yogurt Nonfat Plain (8 oz.)	127	*	*	13	17	5
CHEESE						
American (1 oz.)	106	9	6	6	*	27
Blue (1 oz.)	100	8	5	6	*	21
Brie (1 oz.)	95	8	n/a	6	*	28
Cheddar (1 oz.)	114	9	6	7	*	30
Cheese spread (1 oz.)	87	6	4	5	2	16
Cottage Cheese creamed (½cup)	108	5	3	13	3	16
Cottage Cheese Curd (½cup)	62	*	*	13	1	5
Cottage Cheese 2% fat(½cup)	102	2	1	16	4	9
Cream Cheese (1 oz.)	99	10	6	2	*	31
Gouda (1 oz.)	101	8	5	7	*	32
Gruyere (1 oz.)	117	9	5	8	*	31
Jack (1 oz.)	106	9	n/a	7	*	25
Mozzarella/Whole (1 oz.)	80	6	4	6	*	22
Mozzarella/Skim (1 oz.)	72	5	3	7	*	16
Neufchatel (1 oz.)	74	7	4	3	*	22
Parmesan (1 oz.)	129	9	5	12	1	22
Ricotta Whole (½cup)	214	16	10	14	4	63
Ricotta Skim (½cup)	170	10	6	14	6	38
Roquefort (1 oz.)	105	9	5	6	*	26
Swiss (1 oz.)	107	8	5	8	*	26

Sat=Saturated, Carbs=Carbohydrates,

Choles=Cholesterol, gm=grams, mg=milligrams

* Contains less than 1 gram

PORTION	Calories	Total Fat (Gm)	Sat Fat (Gm)	Protein (Gms)	Carb (Gms)	Choles (Mgs)
FROZEN DESSERTS						
Frozen Yogurt low-fat (½cup)	113	1	n/a	3	23	4
Frozen Yogurt nonfat(½cup)	110	0	0	2	24	0
Ice Cream Rich(½cup)	175	12	7	2	16	44
Ice Cream Low-fat (½cup)	134	7	4	2	16	30
Ice Milk Regular (½cup)	92	3	2	3	14	9
Ice Milk Soft (½cup)	112	2	1	4	19	7
Sherbet (½cup)	135	2	1	1	39	7

Sat=Saturated, Carbs=Carbohydrates,

Choles=Cholesterol, gm=grams, mg=milligrams

* Contains less than 1

LESSON 15: LET'S GET PHYSICAL

In a discussion of the effects of exercise and physical conditioning, it is necessary to differentiate between health and fitness and between fitness and skill. Health in a narrow sense is the absence of disease and more broadly it is the capacity of all body organs and systems to perform high-level functions. Fitness on the other hand relates to performance and survival. Usually, but not always, good fitness requires good health.

Then there is obesity and being overweight. Obesity is a condition where the storage of fat under the skin is excessive, while being overweight is weighing more than the average for your height and age. Being overweight may mean you have unusually heavy bones or well-developed muscles. Reducing the body weight only happens when your energy input is less than your energy output. Thus, a calorie-controlled diet along with exercise can result in loss of weight, but this should be done sensibly. Remember that the reason to reduce is to be healthier. You should consult your doctor before embarking on any drastic die or exercise program and **never** reduce your Calorie intake below 800 calories per day.

Exercise and fitness are terms that have been used interchangeably because their meaning is translated as one and the same. But, fitness is the result of exercising. Next you will review these two terms to clarify the differences.

What Is Exercise?

All living things move. Life is made up of motion going on all around you. The more alive you are, the more you move and enjoy that movement. You walk, run, dance, and move about each day, whether for joy or for work. Well, exercise is motion too and a natural part of your life. Before the invention of cars, trains, elevators and escalators, individuals were able to utilize more of their muscles in just getting around each day. But these wonderful inventions have limited your natural exercise.

Exercise, within the context of this lesson, is the physical training of the body to improve its function. Active exercise is a physical exertion while passive exercise is exercise that involves a machine or the assistance of someone. Physical conditioning is the enhancement of physical fitness through the proper employment of exercise.

Think of exercise as a way of bringing life and vitality to those parts of your body that lie idle during your normal daily activity. Consider exercise to be a beauty treatment for your body to help it retain its limberness and the slimness needed to move gracefully and look youthful.

What Is Fitness?

Fitness may be defined as a combination of physical, mental, and emotional well-being. How well you develop these aspects of your life will determine the quality of your existence. The mere absence of sickness may lead to a classification of being "***HEALTHY***" or being "***WELL***", but physical fitness implies much more. It includes vigor, alertness, and the ability to endure difficult circumstances as well as the energy to enjoy leisure time pursuits.

General physical fitness is the capacity of the body to perform work, to resist disease and infection, and to resist the physical stresses imposed by such things as heat, cold, atmospheric pressure, etc. General physical fitness is the capability of the individual to dominate his usual environment. The degree of fitness is related to the degree of stress that one must be able to overcome.

Who Should Exercise?

Just a few decades ago, many people thought that exercise was for children, that adults should "***SLOW***

DOWN" as they got older. It was assumed that vigorous exercise could hurt the heart, and that people should avoid any strenuous exercise after a heart attack. Today evidence is accumulating that says exercise is not only good, but necessary for health at any age. Exercise, carefully prescribed by a physiologist in conjunction with your physician, can also be a key element in recovering after a heart attack. Therefore, you should be looking at good health as being sound in body and mind, looking good, feeling good, and being free of disease or pain.

Over the last two decades, fitness programs of all kinds have captured the public attention. Americans today are striving to improve their health and appearance and "***working out***" has become the norm. The trend continues, as evidence by recent studies show that 70 percent of the population considers good health the most important thing in life. Included in their perception of good health is the contribution to be made by exercise, sound nutrition and proper health habits.

It is easy to accept the fact that physical conditioning is necessary to achieve and maintain high levels of physical performance. The need for physical fitness among competitive athletes is clear, but why a sedentary person in an industrialized society needs exercise may not be so clear. What does physical fitness mean to the man or woman who needs only to push a button?

What Happens When You Exercise?

Exercise requires energy and energy is derived from foodstuffs stored in the body as fats, proteins, and carbohydrates. When your body goes from a resting condition to one of more intense physical activity, complex physiological changes take place within your body. Changes occur in breathing rate, heart rate, sweating rate and blood pressure with activities such as aerobics, brisk walking, jogging, racquetball, and weight lifting. The responses that you experience are a result of an increase in the physiological functioning of your cardiovascular, respiratory, and metabolic systems. For you to participate in physical activity, or simply to function in daily tasks, there must be a smooth integrated operation of these systems.

Exercise leaves on every organ and system of the body an imprint that persists for several days. This is manifested by improvements shown in subsequent performances and by increased efficiency. The body quickly becomes conditioned to face new physical levels of activity with less tenseness during the effort.

The most obvious change in the body due to physical training is an increase in the strength, size and hardness of the muscles used in exercise. Increase in muscular strength is derived in part from the increase in muscle mass, but in greater part from the better organization of nerve impulses that reach the working muscles at a faster rate and draw them into a stronger contraction.

After a few months of training, muscle enlargement tapers off and the balance tween food intake and energy output of physical activity is accurately revealed by changes in body weight. If food intake exceeds energy output, fat is stored and weight increases. A slight deficit in food intake results in fact and weight loss. It may seem easier to combat obesity by slight starvation rather than by forced exercise because of the large amount of exercises needed to consume an ounce of fat--about one mile of walking, jogging, or running. Weight control by diet alone, however, requires such severe restriction of food intake that it is difficult to obtain the required nutrients--proteins, vitamins, and minerals--and the sparse intake does not satisfy hunger. Therefore, reducing diets often fail.

With added exercise, one does not need to reduce food intake to lose fat, lose weight, and become thinner. Moreover, since exercise, especially before mealtime, lessons the appetite, it is easier to attain a lean body by a combination of increased physical activity and diet restriction.

Muscles

Muscles are the engines of the body. Their job is to move limbs, drive blood around the body, and force food through the digestive tract. Your body weight is made up mostly of muscles and there are more than 600 muscles of different size, shape, and type. The three main muscle types are skeletal, cardiac, and smooth. Skeletal muscles move the head, trunk and limbs and are called voluntary muscles because they usually obey your will. Cardiac muscles operate the heart and are both involuntary and voluntary. Smooth muscles work the stomach, intestines and blood vessels and are sometimes called involuntary because you can't control them. They work automatically.

Muscles consist of long; slim fibers bound in bundles and are called striate or striated muscles. One muscle may be attached to two bones by tough white cords of tissues known as tendons. When a muscle receives an electric signal from a nerve it contracts. The flexor muscles the contraction bends joints and pulls limbs toward the body. The extensor muscles the contraction straightens joints and moves limbs away from the body.

Your muscular system's demand for energy to move

directly influences the supportive efforts of your cardiovascular and respiratory systems. If you exert your muscular system in the proper manner, you're cardiovascular and respiratory systems will improve to easily handle more demanding situations.

The following muscle chart shows the main muscle areas of the body. This is not all the muscles, but the ones usually concentrated on when performing aerobic exercises and muscle building.

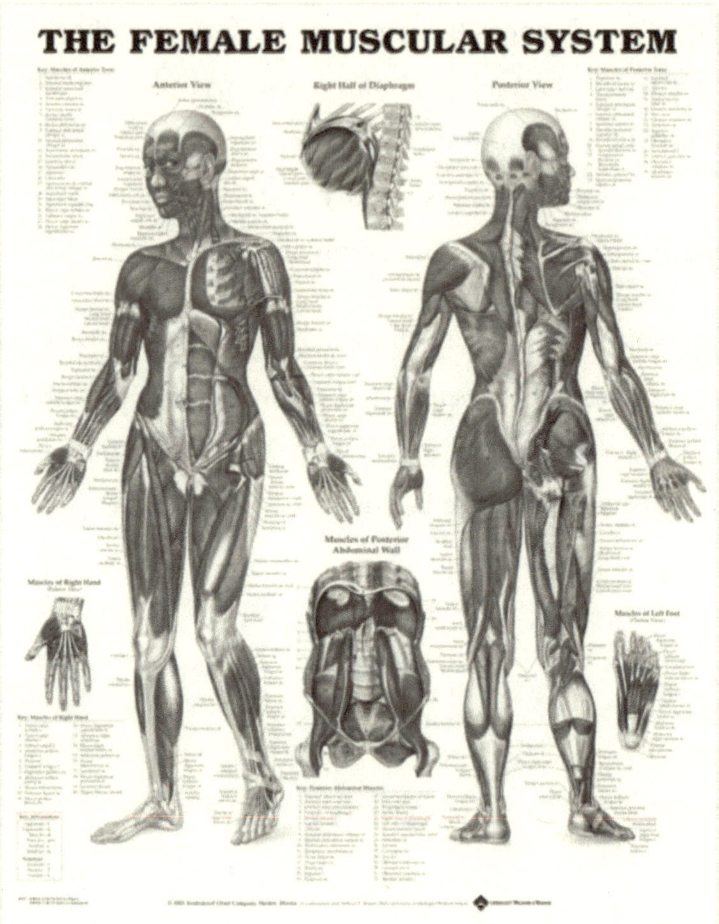

Your muscles work by converting fuel (*nutrients*) to energy. They do this by two different processes.

Anaerobic: Anaerobic involves chemical processes in the muscle that release energy without using oxygen.

Aerobic: Aerobic requires oxygen and is dependent on your cardiovascular system. It depends on your ability to breathe oxygen into your lungs, carry oxygen into the blood, pump it around your body through the action of your heart and blood vessels, and use it in your muscles. The skills involved in aerobic activity makes this the most important form of exercise.

Aerobic exercise uses the large muscle groups in a repetitive and rhythmic action for extended periods of time. The activity should be strenuous enough to increase both your pulse and breathing rate, but not so strenuous that you feel "***breathless***" and unable to continue for prolonged periods.

Among the best aerobic exercises are activities like brisk walking, jogging, swimming, cycling, dancing, and cross-country skiing. Today, aerobics has become its on form of exercise, and aerobic exercise is the only form of exercise that reduces your percentage of body fat.

Exercising For Life

There are those who jump into tights and start exercising the minute they get up, but they are few. Most of you must confess that first think in the morning the only exercise you get is bending your elbow to bring up that first cup of coffee, tea, or milk. For your health as well as for your bodies, you must change your attitude and begin exercising. To give you the incentive, look at the benefits you will gain from exercising:

- It can keep your body younger. People who exercise vigorously on a regular basis have a fitness level equivalent to someone ten to 15 years younger.
- Your cardiovascular efficiency and muscle power will be notably younger if you continue to work out.
- A program of regular exercise promotes better skin tone. Your skin will be more elastic and thicker and less likely to wrinkle.
- Regular exercise promotes and maintains strong bones, thus reducing the risk of osteoporosis (*brittle bones*) when combined with adequate calcium intake.
- Your heart will be stronger, and your circulation will improve.
- The flesh on your body will become firmer.
- You will feel calmer and less stressed by daily activity.

Like anything you do, aerobics take practice to perfect. Once you learn a routine you will develop a flawless ease and grace over time if you put your mind to it. Just remember it is better to do a few exercises perfectly than to do dozens off balance, with jerky movements and lack of grace. It will help if you begin by doing your exercises in front of a full-length mirror. Watch you're every motion carefully and be your own worst critic as you strive for perfection.

Your Exercise Program

Making the personal decision to begin exercise is the first step. Committing to make it a priority in your life is the next. The biggest challenge you will face is changing your lifestyle. You have school work, chores, commitments with the family and fitting in one more thing may seem impossible. You need to make committed effort to consciously recognize and alter some of these patterns so that you can find time to exercise. Less time playing video games, watching TV, or talking on your cell phone might free up some time.

Fat Reduction

Protection of the heart is the main goal of exercise. After the age of 30 you begin to think of fitness as a method of survival. This usually calls for exercise of a different nature from sport. It is estimated that maintenance of a physically active status decreases the chance of coronary heart disease by about a third. Exercise also aids in eliminating other conditions such as obesity and high blood pressure that are among the causes of heart disease.

To enjoy the benefits, exercise should require the

expenditure of at least 300 calories per day and should increase the heart rate above 120 beats per minute for at least three continuous minutes. Such exercise benefits metabolic and cardiovascular functions.

Muscle Strengthening

To increase muscles above 50 percent of their maximum strength is another objective of exercising. Such an increase can be brief; as little as five seconds just once a day. Increased hardness of muscle is due to the greater degree of contraction that can be achieved by bringing more muscle fibers into action. In the relaxed state, the trained muscle is firm but supple, possibly because of its increased ratio of muscle fibers to fat.

Circulatory Adjustment

To stand up for a total of at least two hours every day meets a twofold objective. You will maintain bone structure and preserve orthostatic tone. Orthostatic tone is the adjustment of blood pressure to postural changes that prevent fainting on sudden standing after reclining.

The response of the heart muscle to exercise training is similar to that of skeletal muscle. After such training the heart can contract more strongly and in a better coordinated way so as to wring out more blood with each contraction. In exercising new blood vessels appear in all active tissue, aiding in the delivery of supplies and the removal of waste. There is hardly any increase in the volume of blood to fill these new vessels, but an improved control of pressure provides for a better diversion of blood to active muscles and away from tissues such as the kidneys which tend to shut down during heavy exercise.

Avoidance of Exercise Injuries

Injuries that occur during physical activities are usually the result of forces from outside the body. It is doubtful that a muscle can tear itself by the force of its own contraction. When momentum or resistance is applied suddenly, however, the external force may be added to the internal force of contraction and cause damage. Consider running for instance where the swing of the leg against partially contracted hamstring muscles causes the pulled muscle.

Most exercise injuries involve connective tissue. Muscle pulls usually include injury of the sheets of connective tissue. Sore heels and shin splints are due to traumatic inflammation of the periosteum (the membrane that encloses each bone). Foot and knee pains are frequently ligamentous in origin. You can avoid injuries by progressing gradually from extremely light to heavy training and by using footwear or ground surfaces that absorb the shock of foot striking resistance.

But most of you like to think of exercise as a way to firm and shape your bodies. Exercise will do this for you and it will help you burn calories. Take a look at the chart below.

Calories Burned

ACTIVITY	CALORIES/ MIN	ACTIVITY	CALORIES/ MIN
Aerobics	3.0-10.0	Running	9.0-25.0
Walking	4.0-7.0	Bicycling	4.0-10.0
Jogging	5.0-10.0	Skiing	8.0-16.0
Swimming	6.0-12.0	Step Aerobics	4.0-10.0
Tennis	7.0-11.0	Gymnastics	2.0-6.0

Now that you know what exercise can do for you, it is time to decide on what type of exercise program you will put in place.

Now look at your measurements on your blueprints. Did you find that you had extra inches on areas of your body? If so, these areas will need to be worked so that the next time you ask yourself these questions, you will be happy with the answers.

If like most women, you found that your problem areas are your arms, waist, thighs and hips, aerobic exercise should be made part of your program. Aerobic exercise is the best workout for shaping and toning your body back into the shape it was meant to have. There are other forms of exercise that will help you in trimming excess fat, but when it comes to the waist, abdomen, and hip area, aerobics work best.

You will need to make your own determination of what works best for you. It may be that you need to go to a gym and work out with other individuals or want to design your own program. But whatever you choose, make sure that you stick with your workout, find it interesting and fun to do. For you to stick to it and experience results you must put your heart into it.

There are five areas that should be incorporated in your fitness program and they are:

Warm-up Period: There should be a warm-up at the beginning of the program. In the warm-up there should be stretching and movements to increase your pulse rate. This helps your metabolic system get itself ready for the exercises that follow.

Cool-down Period: There should be a cool-down at the end of the program. Cooling down is very important. While you are exercising an increase amount of blood is being pumped to your heart with the help of contractions in the large leg muscles that press against the veins. If these muscles relax abruptly, the blood collects in your arm and leg areas instead of getting back to your heart which, because of the physical exertion, will be pumping faster but the blood cannot get back up.

Precise Instructions: The instructions should be clearly understandable and give you precise directions that are easy to follow.

Challenging: The exercise routines should be challenging. You want to really feel the movements as you go through the routines. You should continue to challenge your movements to get the most out of them.

Exhilarating: At the end of the work out you should feel exhilarated and able to stand up straighter. You may find that certain parts of your body ache after your workout, but you should feel as though you have grown taller and have the stamina to move gracefully through the day.

Preparation

To prepare to do your work out try to set aside a regular time to exercise. Once you have established this time, turn the phone off before you start so you won't be interrupted. Since you will be working up a sweat, make sure that the place you chose to exercise has no drafts and that the ceiling is high enough to allow you to jump up, or swing your arms out.

You should have an exercise pad or a beach towel to sit on when doing your floor exercises and wear comfortable clothing that will not restrict your movements. The clothing should be loose fitting and comfortable for easy movements, but not baggy. Stretch pants and leotards are excellent. Just as important you should wear a sports bra. Your bra will help support the pectoral muscles and provide protection against tearing down of the delicate tissues around the bust area.

If possible, try to have a big mirror in front of you so that you can see yourself exercising or practice the routines in front of a mirror while concentrating on how your body feels so that you can perform the movement correctly when you are doing your workout.

Having music playing throughout your exercise may not be a necessary component but can turn your exercise time into one of fun and relaxation. Music becomes a companion while you exercise and has a way of sticking in your mind the routine that goes with the music. It is a helpful companion for the workout and you should consider adding it to your program.

One of the most important parts of exercising is how you breathe. Make every movement you do a breathing exercise too. Each time you raise your arms, breathe in.

Each time you lower your arms, breathe out. As you do an exercise that is slow and easy you will get in some very good deep breathing if you concentrate. Coordinating your breathing with your routines will accustom you to better breathing habits in all aspects of your life.

If you have even the slightest trouble with your heart, lungs, back, or legs, or find that you get out of breath quickly or you tire easily, you should have a doctor give you a checkup before you go in for an exercise program.

If you have been leading an inactive life, don't rush suddenly into a heartbreaking, backbreaking routine. Give yourself time. Start with five minutes a day and work up to ten minutes a day in the third week. Keep on increasing until you reach the level you desire, which should be no less than one half hour. You can comfortably peak at one hour or one hour and a half. You will be the judge of when you are ready and how far you should go.

You must discipline yourself to work out at least three times a week, continuously for twenty to thirty minutes at a time. If you have never worked out before, start at this level, and work your way up to one hour a day and strive for six days a week. Include other forms of activities that will keep you from feeling bored with your routine and you will find it easier to accept adding exercise to your daily life. Remember always that this is something you do for yourself and you deserve to give at least a half hour to keeping your body in shape.

You want a program that will give you a good cardiovascular conditioning, endurance, resistance exercises to increase your muscle strength and stretching for flexibility. To achieve true aerobic fitness, you must increase your heart rate to a training level and sustain that level for a minimum of twenty minutes, for at least three times a week.

To determine your training level, you first figure out your maximum heart rate. The maximum rate that a heart can beat is 220 beats a minute. For every year of life, the rate decreases by one beat. So, to get your own maximum heart rate, subtract your age from 220. This will give you a training level representative of between 70 and 85 percent of your maximum heart rate.

To Take Your Pulse

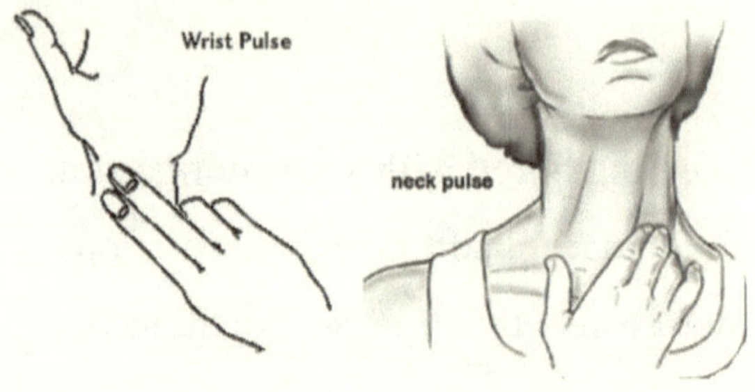

Gently place 2 fingers of your hand on your pulse on the inside of your wrist, below your thumb.

Do not use your thumb, because it has its own pulse that you may feel. You can also check your pulse in the carotid artery. This is in your neck, on either side of your windpipe. Press lightly. Count the number of beats for 15 to 30 seconds and them multiply by four (15 seconds) or two (30 seconds) to find your rate per minute. The following chart presents a guideline.

Normal Pulse	
Age Group	Normal Heart Rate at Rest
Children (ages 6-15)	70-100 beats per minute
Adults (age 18 and over)	60-100 beats per minute

Bear with me! Now comes a lot of math, but it is worth it. You want to take a break before you do all the calcs. Go ahead, I'll wait.

STEP 1: Find your resting heart rate as soon as you

wake up. You can do this by counting your pulse for one minute while still in bed. You may average your heart rate over three mornings to obtain your average resting heart rate (RHR). Add the three readings together and divide that number by three to get the RHR. For example, (60 + 64 + 63) / 3= 62.

STEP 2: Find your maximum heart rate and heart rate reserve by first subtracting your age from 220. This is your maximum heart rate (HRmax). For example, the HRmax for a 14-year-old would be 220 - 14 = 206. Subtract your RHR from your HRmax. This is your heart rate reserve (HRmaxRESERVE). For example, HRmaxRESERVE = 206 - 62 = 144.

STEP 3: Calculate the lower limit of your THR. Figure 60% of the HRmaxRESERVE (multiply by 0.6) and add your RHR to the answer. For example, 144 * 0.6= 86. 86 + 62 = 148

STEP 4: Calculate the upper limit of your THR. Figure 80% of the HRmaxRESERVE (multiply by 0.8) and add your RHR to the answer. For example, (144 * 0.8) + 62 = 177.

STEP 5: Combine the values obtained in steps 3 and 4 and divide by the number 2. For example, (148 + 177) / 2 = 163 (You can get the same result by simply multiplying HRmaxRESERVE by 0.7 and adding to it RHR).

The following chart has been set up representing a 60-75% training level. In using the chart, get your resting heart rate (RHR) and find it on the first row. Then go to your age in the first column and across to your RHR. This will be your ten second target heart rate zone (THR).

If you are younger than the chart, follow Step 1 above to get your Resting Heart Rate.

If AGE	RESTING HEART RATE								
	50	55	60	65	70	75	80	85	90
11-14	24-29	24-28	25-28	25-28	25-29	26-29	26-29	26-29	27-29
15-19	24-28	24-27	25-28	25-28	25-29	26-29	26-29	26-29	27-29
20-24	23-27	23-27	24-28	25-28	25-28	25-28	25-28	26-29	26-29
25-29	23-26	23-27	24-27	24-27	24-27	25-28	25-28	25-28	26-28
30-34	22-26	23-26	23-26	23-26	24-27	24-27	24-27	25-27	25-28
35-39	22-25	22-25	23-26	23-26	23-26	24-26	24-26	24-27	25-27
40-44	21-25	21-24	22-25	22-25	23-25	23-26	23-26	24-26	24-26
45-49	21-24	21-24	21-24	21-24	22-25	23-25	23-25	23-25	23-26
50-54	20-23	21-24	21-24	21-24	22-24	22-25	22-25	23-25	23-25
55-59	20-23	20-23	20-23	21-23	21-24	21-24	22-24	22-24	22-24
60-64	19-22	20-22	20-22	20-23	21-24	21-23	21-23	22-24	22-24
65-69	19-21	19-22	19-22	20-22	20-22	20-23	21-23	21-23	21-23
70-74	18-21	19-21	19-21	19-21	20-22	20-22	20-22	21-22	21-22
75-79	18-20	18-20	18-21	19-21	19-21	19-21	20-21	20-22	20-22
80-85	17-20	18-20	18-20	18-20	19-20	19-21	19-21	20-21	20-21

To find your exercise heart rate, monitor your pulse for

10 seconds immediately following aerobic exercise. Look at the chart above and if your exercise heart rate falls within the target heart rate zone you are doing fine, but if it is above, decrease the intensity of your workout. If it falls below, increase your exercise intensity. To If you are just starting out, seek a 60 percent level and work your way up gradually until your training level falls between 70 and 85 percent of your maximum heart rate.

Making Your Choice

Exercise can be grouped into four basic categories of light, moderate, strenuous, and static. Light exercise can be continued for hours and the heart rate seldom exceeds 110 beats per minute and breathing rate is usually less than 17 per minute. The chemical changes produced by muscular contractions proceed apace and the blood constituents remained undisturbed. Walking, bowling, archery, baseball, woodworking, and housekeeping would fall into this category.

A few minutes of moderate exercise is tiring unless you are well conditioned. During moderate exercise the heart rate is around 120 beats per minute and the breathing rate is about 18 per minute. Blood changes are slight or nonexistent. Jogging, golf, basketball, football, downhill skiing, and skating are examples of moderate exercise.

Strenuous exercise can be endured only for a few seconds. The heart rate exceeds 130 per minute and respiration is faster than 20 per minute. The chemical residues of muscle activity accumulate as acids in the blood. Within five minutes the non-athlete is exhausted. Running at near-maximum speeds, wrestling, fast rowing, speed swimming, gymnastics and shoveling snow fall in this category.

Static exercise involves holding a stressful position. The fatigue felt during the performance of static exercise is confined to the involvement of muscles. When such static exercise is continued beyond one minute, the heart, lungs and chemical processes are severely stressed. Gymnastics, weight lifting are examples of static exercise.

Look over the types of exercise that follow. Your first step is to decide how fit you want to be then what type of exercise fits your life style. Whatever level of fitness you wish to attain and however you choose to maintain it, you should try for a balanced program of mobility, strengthening and heart and lung exercises for total fitness. Choose the activities most suited to your needs and remember that your choice should be what you enjoy doing. Also, it is wise to check with your doctor before beginning any strenuous exercise.

Mobility Exercises

Exercise movements that ensure that all the major joints and muscles are moved through their complete range of movement. Think of this type of exercise as good for office workers, dancers, sport addicts, runners, and weight lifters. This type of exercise promotes mobility and flexibility and includes yoga as well as any exercises involving bending, stretching, and rotating movements.

Mobility exercise will help loosen stiff joints and muscles and promote smoothness and ease of movement.

Activities such as sports, swimming, golf, gymnastics, squash, athletics, aerobics, and calisthenics fall in this category.

Strength Exercises

Good for everyone. They give the body muscles shape and tone and aid self-confidence. It prepares the body for coping with situations calling for extra effort such as carrying suitcases or changing a tire. It helps the muscles and therefore is good for people doing heavy manual work as it builds up the weight and strength of the muscles by means of repeated actions.

Strength exercises include skiing, shot put, swimming, wrestling and strength/endurance exercises such as push-ups, squat jumps, and sit-ups.

Heart and Lung Exercises

Improves the performance and endurance of the cardiovascular (circulatory) and respiratory systems. These types of exercises will benefit anyone seeking to improve general fitness as they increase the oxygen requirements of the body. They require continued vigorous movement over an extended period.

Heart and lung exercises include racquet ball, football, running, jogging, skipping, cycling, cross-country skiing, and swimming.

Isometric Exercises

These are exercises without movement. The muscles are put into a state of static contraction of force against the resistance of muscles. This type of exercise is used to increase muscle strength and can be done everywhere. Isometrics do not improve cardiovascular performance and should be added to a program that provides this type of workout.

Isotonic Exercises

Exercise with movements using the body against itself or against weight. It includes calisthenics but basically is considered to be a weight training or bodybuilding exercise. This type of exercise will increase the size, strength and endurance as weights are varied to suit the individual. Isotonic exercise can be suitable for everyone and should be performed with stretching exercises to loosen the muscles. A cardiovascular program should also be made part of your program for the best benefits.

Isokinetic Exercises

These are resistance exercises that are combined with the principle of both isometric and isotonic exercises. It involves the use of equipment that controls the amount of resistance relative to the degree of exertion and is excellent for increasing the size and strength of muscles. This type of exercise has little or no added cardiovascular exercise and should be done in conjunction with aerobic or stretching exercises.

Aerobics

Aerobic is a form of exercise that works all parts of the body, incorporating a good cardiovascular workout. Aerobics are usually done to music and are classified as low and high impact. In 1986, Gin Miller implemented the concept of step training and the demand for this total body workout was received with enthusiasm. Step aerobics gives an excellent cardiovascular workout with low level of mechanical stress on the feet. This as well as regular aerobics which is done on a flat surface with rhythmical routines performed while standing and then laying on the floor. Step aerobics can provide the cardiovascular benefits of running at 7 mph and the exertion on the feet is in line with walking 3 mph.

Other Exercises

Meditative exercise such as yoga, K'ai Men and T'ai Chi are all good for.muscular tone, overall flexibility, internal functions, and stress relief. They have little or no cardiovascular value but are an excellent addition to an aerobic program.

Sports such as tennis, golf and team sports can increase the incentive to exercise and make it more enjoyable.

Saunas and steam baths do not improve fitness or maintain it, but temporary loss of weight may result from the loss of water through sweating. They do help to relax the muscles and to tone and deeply cleanse the skin, while also helping to relax the nervous system and relieve tension. As far as exercise is concerned, they have no effect whatsoever.

Massages do not aid fitness or provide exercise in any way. Massages relax the muscles, reduce mental tension, improve the flow of blood and lymph, stretch muscle fibers and can be very enjoyable.

Duration And Frequency Of Exercise

The American College of Sports Medicine recommends that an aerobic segment of exercise be 20 to 60 minutes in duration, but usually it will run between 20-30 minutes. Frequency of exercising usually falls between three to five times per week, but to minimize stress on the joints and bones it is suggested to incorporate aerobics on alternate days during the initial conditioning stages.

The person who has been idle for years does not benefit from a "crash" attempt to make up for lost years of exercising by exhaustive regimen. This can do more harm than good. After a long layoff, before exercise is undertaken a medical examination that includes an evaluation of response to exercise is prudent. According to specialists in sports medicine, it is more important for a person to seek medical advice before deciding to become inactive as the risks to health are greater than deciding to step up the level of exercise.

A reconditioning regimen that commences at an easy level for a brief period of five minutes will produce cardiovascular, neuromuscular, and metabolic benefits at any age and for persons in the poorest of physical condition this would be the way to begin. You should seek a heart rate level of 100 beats per minute during the first month of exercising. During the month the duration of daily exercise can be extended from the starting point of five minutes to ten minutes.

The second month seek to advance the heart rate to 110 per minute if no discomfort appears and move up to 120 per minute heart rate during the third month. On days when the exercise does not feel comfortable, stop, and repeat the same program the following day.

When To Exercise

When to exercise is usually a personal preference, but the following will help you in making this decision.

Mornings: Exercising in the morning requires a warming-up period to arouse the body from sleep. It can be an excellent time to work out and allows the rest of the day free to pursue what needs to get done.

Afternoons: Works out well in breaking up the day, especially if there are facilities nearby. It can prevent afternoon tiredness and boredom and helps with dieting as exercising before a meal can help you to reduce, diverting blood from the digestive tract and thus relieving feelings of hunger.

Evenings: Often said to be the best time to exercise as it rids the body of the day's tension and relaxes the body for sleep.

The following will give you the details you need to keep in mind while doing your exercises and may help you in making your choice for the program that will make you fit for life.

To eliminate serious injury, you should consult a doctor if you experience any of the following problems:

- Dizziness, lightheaded, loss of coordination, confusion, cold sweat, glassy stare, pallor, blueness, or fainting.
- Irregular or racing pulse, very slow pulse after training, fluttering, pumping or palpitations in the chest, pain or pressure in the arm or throat.
- Rapid heart rate, breathless, nausea or vomiting, or prolonged fatigue
- Side stitches, cramps, pain in joints or muscle strain.

In general, when doing any time of exercise try and follow these seven points:

POINT 1: Keep shoulders back, chest up, buttocks tucked under the hips and the knees soft.

POINT 2: Do not hyper-extend or bend forward from the waist as is places excess strain on your lower back.

POINT 3: Never flex the knee beyond 90 degrees when it is bearing weight. If you have chronic knee problems, do not flex beyond 60 degrees.

POINT 4: Avoid locking the knee joint

POINT 5: Lean your full body forward, from the ankle joint and not bending the back.

POINT 6: Always lift using the legs and not the back or arms and when lifting, keep the weight close to the body.

POINT 7: Keep your body hydrated by drinking cold water throughout the workout.

Aerobic Pointers

When doing any aerobic exercise program, whether it is one that you set up for yourself, or one you purchase or perform at a gym, your first point of business is a program that works every part of your body--arms, neck, bust, waist, abdomen, hips, buttocks, thighs, calves, ankles--including all areas of these parts (*inside thighs, outside thighs, left and right side of waist, inside arm, outside arm, etc.*). You want your whole body to be able to perform in unison; therefore, you need to work all areas of the body in a good aerobic exercise program.

When doing the exercises, you should:

- Point your toes by arching your foot till it achieves the long, pointed appearance of the ballet dancer at her most graceful arch.
- Flex your foot so that it is pulled up toward your calve in a flat "stepping" position.
- Keep knees absolutely straight when the exercise calls for your knees to be straight.
- Bend knees "slightly" as the exercise calls for a slightly bent knee.
- Keep your head high, erect, symmetrically balanced.
- Bend neck forward, backward, sideways, etc. as far as you can and with controlled movements.
- Pull each muscle until you feel the muscle that you are working on during a routine.
- Expend energy and emphasize each movement like an individual part of a dance routine.
- Breathe in and breathe out in deep lung filling breathes and hold until told to release.

- Concentrate on each movement and breathing in or out as the repetition instructs you to do. Breathing is very important during any kind of exercise.
- Try not to stop during an aerobic routine until you have completed the full exercise session.

If you are just starting out, try to do a complete program of one half hour. Then, once you are comfortable with the one-half hour routine, advance yourself up to one hour of exercise. This can be your leveling off point and will provide you with adequate exercise. Some may want to try for a ninety-minute routine which can be even more beneficial.

Bodybuilding Pointers

Few people who read this book will want to develop massive biceps or become a future Ms. Universe, but a good bodybuilding program will increase physical strength and improve physical appearance.

If you are interested in bodybuilding for a better, firmer body, consider isometric, calisthenics, isokinetic or weight training which differs from weight lifting.

You should keep in mind the following:

- The room should be well ventilated but quite

warm, at least 65 to 70 degrees.

- Work out in front of a mirror to check that you are doing the exercises correctly.
- A sensible program would consist of 15 minutes of exercise on alternate days.
- Always limber up with some simple exercises before using weights and after your workout take a warm shower.
- Never exercise immediately after eating. Instead wait an hour and don't eat directly after exercising, wait a half hour.
- Eat a well-balanced, nutritious diet that is high in proteins, carbohydrates, vitamins, minerals and includes plenty of liquids and roughage.
- Start with the lightest weights and the simplest exercises doing up to 8 or 10 repetitions and gradually build up to 20 or 30.
- Wear warm clothing such as a track suit to keep the muscles warm.
- Always lift weights with your sternum pushed up to keep pressure off the back.

Running Pointers

If you decide to add running or jogging to your exercise program it should be with care and caution. You should consider the following points.

- Invest in a good pair of running shoes and wear socks to absorb some of the pressure.
- Wear comfortable clothing when you run or jog.
- Run with music as it stimulates the nervous system.
- Start slowly, stretch before and after running. Start out running a couple of hundred yards.
- Twenty to thirty minutes a day, four days a week is sufficient to get the benefits of running.
- If you become tired or winded, walk for a while. When you feel rested do another couple of hundred yards. When you reach a half, a mile quit if you don't want to do more.
- You should aim to work up to two, three or four miles at a time.
- If you experience soreness or fatigue, slow your progress down.
- Monitor your body closely to see how it's responding.

Exercise Machine Pointers

When using machines in your exercise programs, whether they are powered or manual you should do the following:

- Always stretch the muscles before getting on the machine.

- Take your time and follow the recommended procedures for use of the equipment.
- Start slowly and for short periods of time and work up to the recommended periods suggested by the manufacturer.
- Wear loose clothing and either have a TV or radio to help keep you going so that you don't become bored.
- At the end of your work out, stretch again before you shower.

Developing Your Exercise Program

To help you get started, the following exercise program will help you get into shape. Starting now, begin performing the exercises at least three times a week and work yourself up to every day. Don't forget the pointers and instructions on proper performance of exercises. Put on a favorite record with a medium to fast beat and get ready to begin.

How to warm up before exercising

Warm up properly before exercising to prevent injury and make your workouts more effective. This warm-up routine should take at least 6 minutes. Warm up for longer if you feel the need.

MARCH ON THE SPOT – KEEP GOING FOR 3 MINUTES

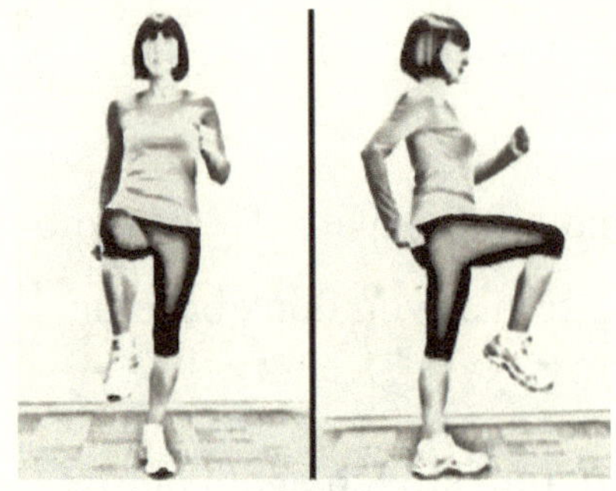

Start off marching on the spot and then march forwards and backwards. Pump your arms up and down in rhythm with your steps, keeping the elbows bent and the fists soft.

HEEL DIGS – AIM FOR 60 HEEL DIGS IN 60 SECONDS

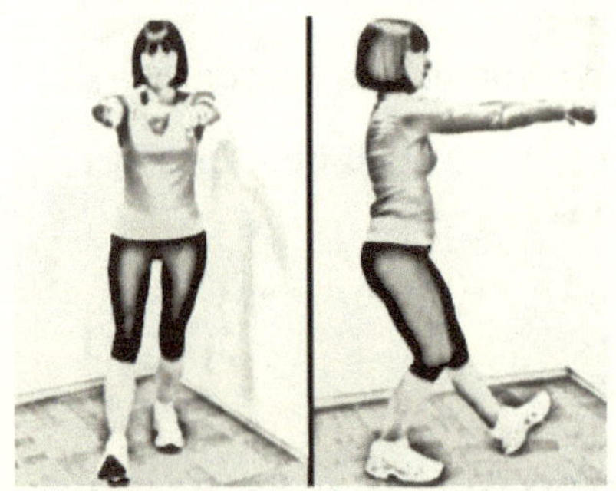

For heel digs, place alternate heels to the front, keeping the front foot pointing up, and punch out with each heel dig. Keep a slight bend in the supporting leg.

Knee Lifts – Aim for 30 Knee Lifts in 30 Seconds

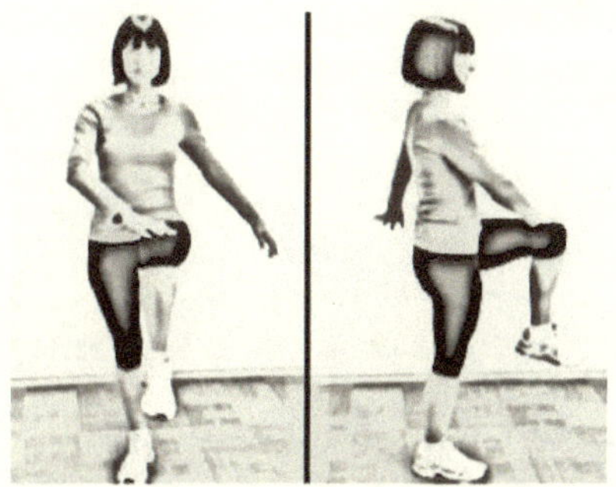

To do knee lifts, stand tall, bring up alternate knees to touch the opposite hand. Keep your abdominal muscles tight and back straight. Keep a slight bend in the supporting leg.

Shoulder Rolls – 2 Sets of 10 Repetitions

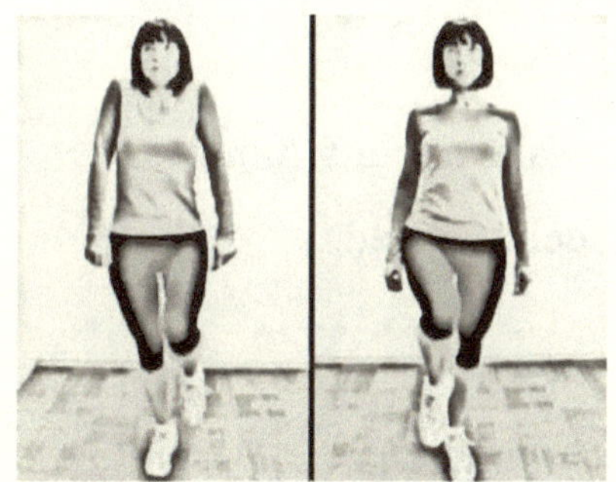

For shoulder rolls, keep marching on the spot. Roll your shoulders forwards 5 times and backwards 5 times. Let your arms hang loose by your sides.

KNEE BENDS – 10 REPETITIONS

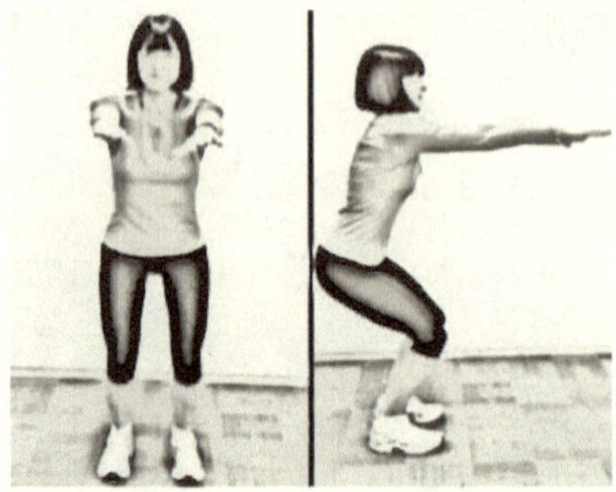

To do knee bends, stand with your feet shoulder-width apart and your hands stretched out. Lower yourself no more than 10cm by bending your knees. Come up and repeat.

How to stretch after exercising

How to stretch and cool down after a workout to gradually relax, improve flexibility and slow your heart rate.

This cool-down routine should take about 5 minutes. Spend more time on it if you feel the need.

BUTTOCK STRETCH – HOLD FOR 10 TO 15 SECONDS

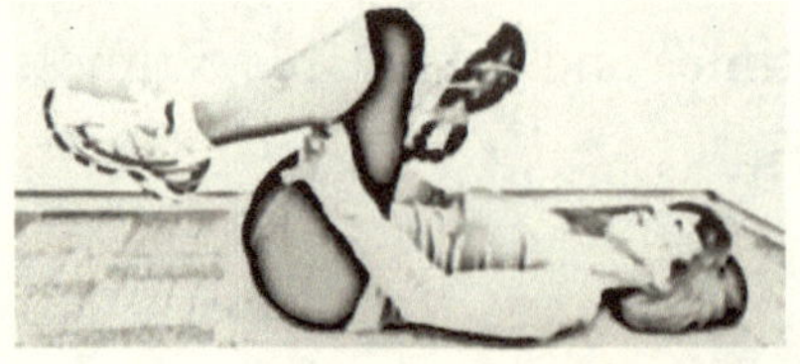

To do a buttock stretch, bring knees up to chest. Cross right leg over left thigh. Grasp back of left thigh with both hands. Pull left leg toward chest. Repeat with opposite leg.

HAMSTRING STRETCH – HOLD FOR 10 TO 15 SECONDS

To do a hamstring stretch, lie on your back, and raise your right leg. Keeping your left leg bent with your foot on the floor, pull your right leg towards you keeping it straight. Don't hold at the knee level. Repeat with opposite leg.

INNER THIGH STRETCH – HOLD FOR 10 TO 15 SECONDS

For the inner thigh stretch, sit down with your back straight and bend your legs, putting the soles of your feet together. Holding on to your feet, try to lower your knees towards the floor.

CALF STRETCH – HOLD FOR 10 TO 15 SECONDS

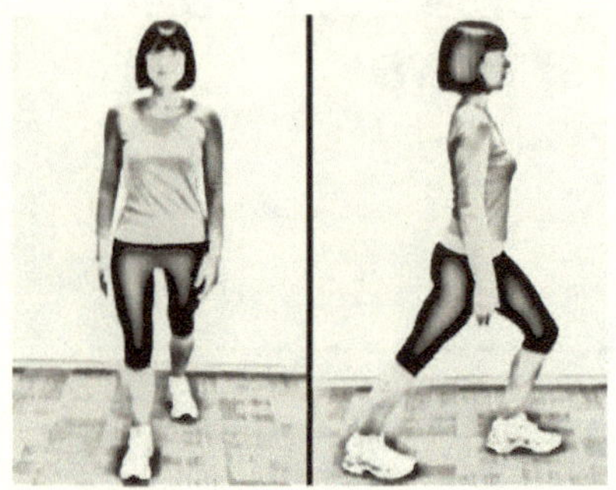

For the calf stretch, step your right leg forward, keeping it bent and lean forwards slightly. Keep your left leg straight and try to lower the left heel to the ground. Repeat with opposite leg.

THIGH STRETCH – HOLD FOR 10 TO 15 SECONDS

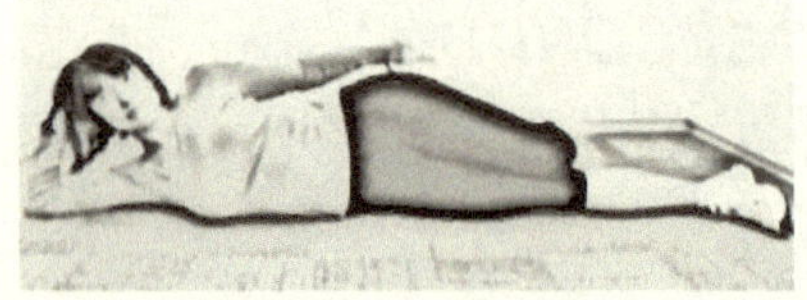

To do a thigh stretch, lie on right side. Grab top of left foot and gently pull heel towards left buttock to stretch the front of the thigh, keeping knees touching. Repeat on the other side.

10-minute home cardio workout

ROCKET JUMPS – 2 SETS OF 15 TO 24 REPETITIONS (REPS)

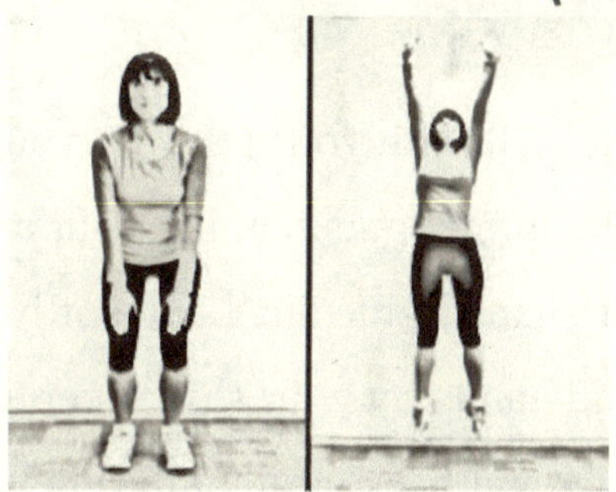

For rocket jumps, stand with your feet hip-width apart, legs bent and hands on your thighs. Jump up, driving your hands straight above your head and extending your entire body. Land softly, reposition your feet and repeat.

For more of a challenge, start in a lower squat position and hold a weight or a bottle of water in both hands at the center of your chest.

- Recovery: walk or jog on the spot for 15 to 45 seconds.

STAR JUMPS OR SQUATS – 2 SETS OF 15 TO 24 REPS

To do a star jump, stand tall with your arms by your side and knees slightly bent. Jump up, extending your arms and legs out into a star shape in the air. Land softly, with your knees together and hands by your side. Keep your abdominal muscles tight and back straight during the exercise.

SQUATS

As a less energetic alternative, do some squats. Stand with your feet shoulder-width apart and your hands down by your sides or stretched out in front for extra balance. Lower yourself by bending your knees until they are at a right angle, with your thighs parallel to the floor. Keep your back straight and don't let your knees extend over your toes.

- Recovery: walk or jog on the spot for 15 to 45 seconds.

Tap backs – 2 sets of 15 to 24 reps

To start tap backs, step your right leg back and swing both arms forward and repeat with the opposite leg in a continuous rhythmic movement. Look forwards and keep your hips and shoulders facing forwards. Don't let your front knee extend over your toes as you step back.

For more of a challenge switch legs by jumping, also known as spotty dog, remembering to keep the knees soft as you land. Your back heel needs to be off the floor always.

- Recovery: walk or jog on the spot for 15 to 45

seconds.

BURPEES – 2 SETS OF 15 TO 24 REPS

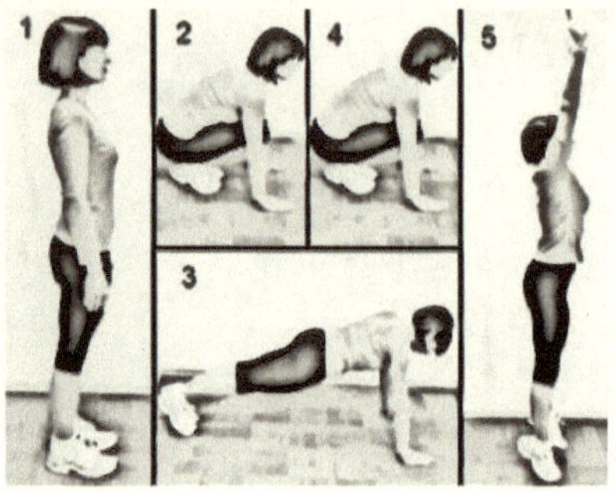

To do a burpee (1), from a standing position, (2) drop into a squat with your hands on the ground. (3) Kick your feet back into a push-up position. (4) Jump your feet back into a squat and (5) jump up with your arms extending overhead. For an easier burpee, don't kick out into the push-up position and stand up instead of jumping.

Now cool down with a 5-minute stretch and cool-down routine.

SQUATS – GREAT FOR FIRM BUMS AND THIGHS

Stand with your feet shoulder-width apart and your hands down by your sides or stretched out in front for extra balance. Lower yourself by bending your knees until they are at a right angle, with your thighs parallel to the floor. Keep your back straight and don't let your knees extend over your toes.

- perform 2 sets of 15 to 24 repetitions (reps)

LUNGES – GREAT FOR FIRM BUMS AND THIGHS

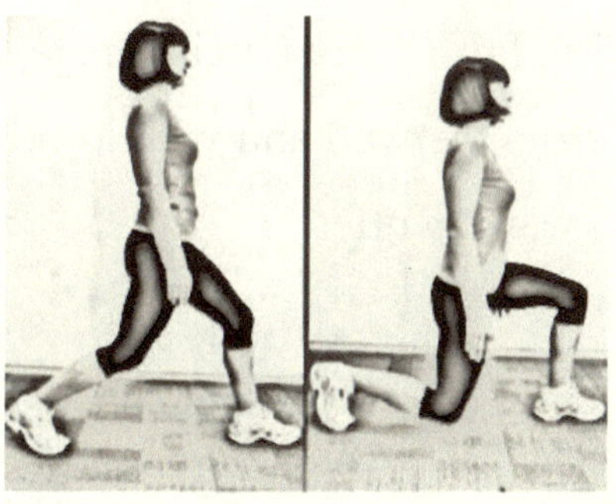

Stand in a split stance with your right leg forward and left leg back. Slowly bend the knees, lowering into a lunge until both legs are at right angles. Keeping the weight in your heels, push back up to starting position. Keep your back straight and don't let your knees extend over your toes.

- 1 set of 15 to 24 reps with each leg

CALF RAISES – GREAT FOR SHAPELY LEGS AND CALVES

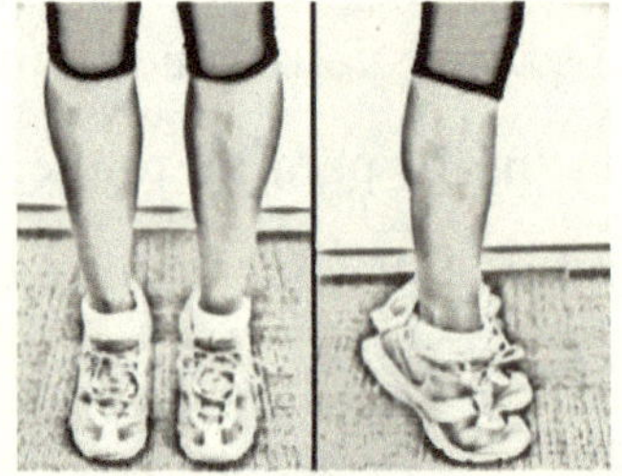

Stand straight but avoid locking your legs. Slowly move onto your toes lifting your heels off the ground and then slowly lower your heels back down. Place hands on a wall or chair for stability. For more of a challenge, do these calf raises away from the wall and with a weight in each hand, such as two water bottles.

- 2 sets of 15 reps

BRIDGES – GREAT FOR FIRM BUMS

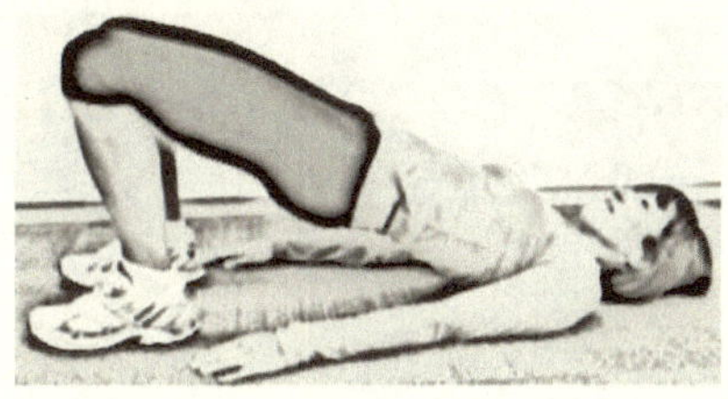

Lie on your back with your knees bent and heels close to your bottom. Your feet should be shoulder-width apart and flat on the floor. Raise your hips up to create a straight line from knees to shoulders. As you come up, tighten your abdominal and buttock muscles. Don't let your knees point outwards.

- 2 sets of 15 to 20 reps

STOMACH CRUNCHES – GREAT FOR STRONG ABS

Lie down on your back, knees bent and hands behind your ears. Keeping your lower back pressed into the floor, raise your shoulder blades no more than 3 inches off the floor and slowly lower down. Don't tuck your neck into your chest as you rise and don't use your hands to pull your neck up.

- 2 sets of 15 to 24 reps

OBLIQUES – GREAT FOR TONING LOVE HANDLES

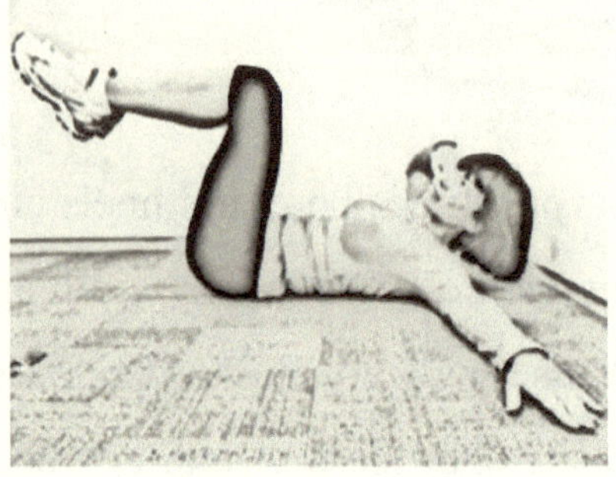

Lie down on your back with your knees bent and together and feet off the floor. Place your right hand behind your right ear and extend the left arm out. Keeping your lower back pressed into the floor, lift your shoulder blades off the floor and curl your upper body diagonally across your chest towards your left knee and lower down.

- 1 set of 12 to 24 reps on each side

BACK RAISES – GREAT FOR GOOD POSTURE

Lie down on your chest and place your hands by your temples or extended out in front for more of a challenge. Keeping your legs together and feet on the ground, raise your shoulders off the floor no more than 3 inches and slowly lower down. Keep a long neck and look down as you perform the exercise.

- 2 sets of 15 to 24 reps

Squat – 2 sets of 15 to 24 reps

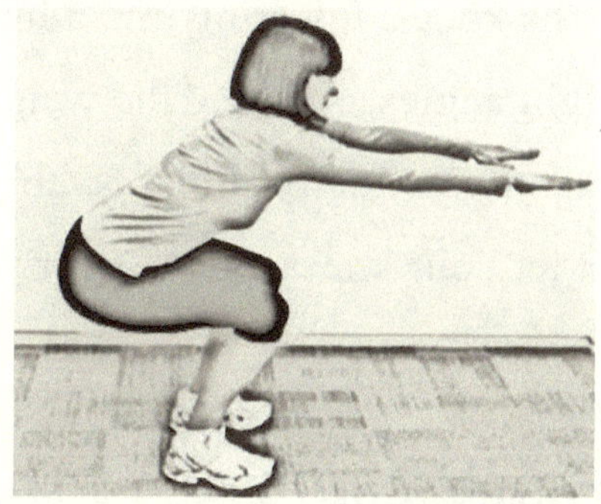

Stand with your feet shoulder-width apart and your hands down by your sides or stretched out in front for extra balance. Lower yourself by bending your knees until they are at a right angle, with your thighs parallel to the floor. Keep your back straight and don’t let your knees extend over your toes.

Lunge – 1 set of 15 to 24 reps with each leg

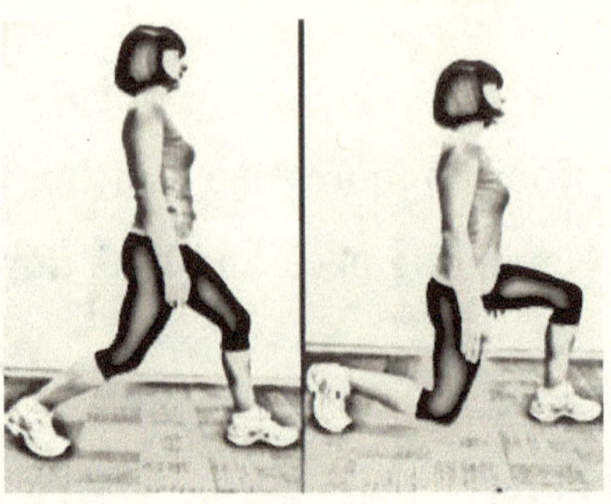

Stand in a split stance with your right leg forward and left leg back. Slowly bend the knees, lowering into a lunge until both legs are at right angles. Keeping the weight in your heels, push back up to starting position. Keep your back straight and don't let your knees extend over your toes.

Stomach crunch – 2 sets of 15 to 24 reps

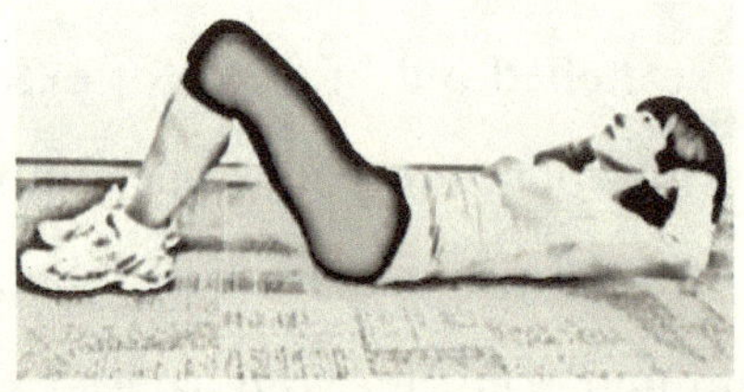

Lie down on your back, knees bent and hands behind your ears. Keeping your lower back pressed into the floor, raise your shoulder blades no more than 3 inches off the floor and slowly lower down. Don't tuck your neck into your chest as you rise and don't use your hands to pull your neck up.

10-minute abs workout

STOMACH CRUNCH

Lie on your back, knees bent and feet flat on the floor, hip-width apart. Place your hands on your thighs, across your chest or behind your ears. Slowly curl up towards your knees until your shoulders are about three inches off the floor. Hold the position for a few seconds and lower down slowly. Perform 12 stomach crunches.

- Don't tuck your neck into your chest as you rise.
- Contract your abdominal muscles throughout the exercise.
- Don't yank your head off the floor.

OBLIQUE CRUNCH

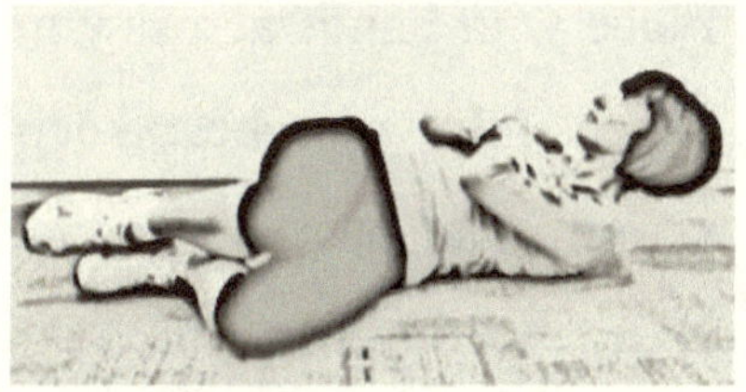

Lie on your back, knees bent and feet flat on the floor, hip-width apart. Roll your knees to one side down to the floor. Place your hands across your chest or behind your ears. Slowly curl up towards your hips until your shoulders are about three inches off the floor. Hold the position for a few seconds and lower down slowly. Perform 12 oblique crunches and repeat on the opposite side.

- Don't tuck your neck into your chest as you rise.
- Contract your abdominal muscles throughout the exercise.
- Don't yank your head off the floor.

STOMACH CRUNCH WITH LEGS RAISED

Lie on your back with your knees bent and feet flat on the floor, hip-width apart. Place your hands across your chest. Slowly pull your knees into your chest, keeping them bent at 90 degrees, until your buttocks and tailbone come off the floor. Hold the position for a moment and lower down slowly. Perform 12 crunches.

- Contract your abdominals throughout the exercise.

- Don't tuck your neck into your chest as you rise.
- Don't use your hands to pull your neck up.

How To Reduce Or Gain

Only if your energy input is less than your energy output will you get thinner. A calorie-controlled diet that incorporates the limiting of fats will be the most beneficial in weight loss, along with exercise. You will be wise to consult your doctor before embarking on a drastic diet and never go below 800 calories per day. If your aim is to lose weight, you will need an exercise program that requires physical exertion plus a sensible diet that decreases your normal amount of calorie intake.

The key to shaping your figure through exercise is as follows:

For Spot Reducing: Perform the exercise at a ***FAST*** tempo. This does not mean that you must rush through them, but that the pace is a rapid one, yet permits you to perform the motions of each exercise fully. Do not attempt to speed up the routine by cutting corners.

For Spot Gaining: Perform the exercise at a ***SLOW*** tempo that resembles how you would feel if you were part of a slow-motion picture. This is the secret to building up those softly rounded, firm, feminine curves that you wish to attain.

You can incorporate spot exercises for certain areas of your body to improve their shape. Spot exercises are not to be your total exercise program. Spot exercises are in addition to your regular work out. Or you can add these on to your daily workout. Do not waste the time you spend getting yourself into top notch physical shape by not working your full body.

Charting Your Progress

Review your Self-Analysis charts and begin filling in the information requested on the Body Profile Chart. Be sure to fill the chart totally, so that you will know what your goals are in each area. In filling out the "*Body Profile Charts*" the increase and/or decrease column should be used to record the number of inches you wish to either increase or decrease. For decreases in an area, put the figure in parenthesis. After a period retake your measurements (***one to two months***) and note "**Yes**" or "**No**". If still require further change, fill in the next chart. Three charts are supplied for your use. If you find you require more sheets, make a copy before filling in the last one to continue your analysis. In filling out the remaining charts "*Charting Your Exercise Program*", you will be recording your exercise benefits for a ten-week period. You will place a check under the day of the week for the areas you have worked so that you have a record of what you have done for each part of your body. When you reach the halfway point, it would be a good time to recheck your body measurements and note any improvement on the "Body Profile Chart.".

Remember, to achieve health, vitality, flexibility, and figure shaping you need to use a good exercise program that includes stretching, cardiovascular routines, aerobics, and a cool down. You should strive to work out at least three days per week and try to increase to six days per week. It is also important that you start out slowly and increase the time of your workout. Usually it is safe to start at 20 to 30 minutes and work your way up to one hour per day.

Take your time and make sure that you do the exercises properly. A few routines done correctly will bring you benefits, while a few routines not performed correctly may only serve to hurt you.

Exercise is important and worth taking the time to do them well. You will thank yourself each day as you begin to see results in the way you walk, how you feel and realize that you are both mentally and physically stronger.

Body Profile Chart

	CHECK ONE		IMPROVEMENT	
SELF ANALYSIS	GOOD	BAD	YES	NO
POSTURE				

BODY PROFILE	MEASUREMENTS			IMPROVE MENT	
	Present	Desired	Increase/ Decrease	Yes	No
Chin					
Neck					
Shoulders					
Arms					
Bust					
Spine					
Waist					
Abdomen					
Hips					
Buttocks					
Thighs					
Knees					
Calves					
Ankles					

NOTE: For *Increase/Decrease* column, record number of inches to increase or decrease for the area. For decreases, put the figure in parentheses. At the end of the fifth week, retake your measurements and note whether you have had any improvements (***Yes*** or ***No*** column). If you still require more time to reach your goal, continue and fill in the next chart. Three charts are supplied for your use. If you require more, make a copy before filling in the last.

Body Profile Chart

	CHECK ONE		IMPROVEMENT	
SELF ANALYSIS	GOOD	BAD	YES	NO
POSTURE				

BODY PROFILE	MEASUREMENTS			IMPROVEMENT	
	Present	Desired	Increase/ Decrease	Yes	No
Chin					
Neck					
Shoulders					
Arms					
Bust					
Spine					
Waist					
Abdomen					
Hips					
Buttocks					
Thighs					
Knees					
Calves					
Ankles					

NOTE: For *Increase/Decrease* column, record number of inches to increase or decrease for the area. For decreases, put the figure in parentheses. At the end of the fifth week, retake your measurements and note whether you have had any improvements (***Yes*** or ***No*** column). If you still require more time to reach your goal, continue and fill in the next chart. Three charts are supplied for your use. If you require more, make a copy before filling in the last.

Body Profile Chart

	CHECK ONE		IMPROVEMENT	
Self-Analysis	Good	Bad	Yes	No
Posture				

Body Profile	Measurements			Improvement	
	Present	Desired	Increase/ Decrease	Yes	No
Chin					
Neck					
Shoulders					
Arms					
Bust					
Spine					
Waist					
Abdomen					
Hips					
Buttocks					
Thighs					
Knees					
Calves					
Ankles					

NOTE: For *Increase/Decrease* column, record number of inches to increase or decrease for the area. For decreases, put the figure in parentheses. At the end of the fifth week, retake your measurements and note whether you have had any improvements (***Yes*** or ***No*** column). If you still require more time to reach your goal, continue by creating a copy of the following chart in a notebook.

Charting Your Exercise Program

Exercise Program Should Include	Program Performance Each Week													
	____ Week							____ Week						
	M	T	W	T	F	S	S	M	T	W	T	F	S	S
Stretch/Workout														
Abdomen (Lower)														
Abdomen (Upper)														
Ankles(Tendons)														
Arms (Inside)														
Arms (Outside)														
Back (Lower)														
Back (Upper)														
Feet														
Hands														
Hips (Back														
Hips (Side)														
Legs (Inside)														
Legs (Outside)														
Neck														
Thighs (Inner														
Thighs (Outer)														
Waist														
Wrists														
Cardiovascular														
Aerobics														
Weight Lifting														
Sports														
Running/Jogging														
Cool Down														

LESSON 16: FINDING YOUR FASHION PASSION

Fashion is a phenomenon that has been puzzling sociologists and psychologists for years and fashion has been going in cycles ever since people began wearing clothes.

Over the years there have been radical changes in women's and men's fashions. How much has changed can be identified by looking at your family photo album and seeing the styles that have come and gone. Talking to people older than you will also enlighten the fact that not only do styles constantly change, but some come back again. If you dig a little further, you may hear people saying that in their closets are clothes they never had a chance to wear out or other items of clothing they are too partial to and can't seem to let go. Now you should be able to sense that keeping up with the latest trend in fashion can be costly and can prove disappointing if you don't know how to plan a wardrobe that will stay in style for longer periods of time.

How can you do this? The secret lies in knowing and understanding the trends of the current styles, adapting them to you and then developing your own style. But what is your own style, you might ask. You are about to learn that style in your wardrobe is as personal as all other areas of your self-development. From this point on you should think of clothing as accents to your figure, hair, skin and even your features. You should think of styling your wardrobe as something you consider not only taste, but also your personal make up. Once you have determined what works best for you, it then becomes necessary to go one step further and begin learning how to recognize a basic style as opposed to a seasonal fashion change.

A basic style will last from seven to eight years while a seasonal change is merely a variation on the basic theme or trend. In a practical sense, anything that is less than seven or eight years old in your closet still has some fashion life left in it.

What you will be learning in this section is how to paint a very personal picture of you with clothes that bring out your personality and your individuality. The knowledge you develop will allow you to work with what you have and leave the high fashion field to those that can afford it. Just by the addition of accessories and minor changes to your basic wardrobe you can achieve an updated "look" that works for you.

Improving Your Fashion Sense

The first step in improving your fashion sense is in knowing that the impression you make on others by the way you look is immediate and irreversible. People react to these impressions in an instinctive, involuntary way. At a quick glance, most people make estimates about profession, dependability, authority, friendliness, competence, and intelligence. Those you know well and those you meet in your work environment form their impressions on the image you portray before you ever open your mouth. Your appearance, then, becomes a voluntary or involuntary estimate of your authority, your efficiency, and your trustworthiness. It may not seem fair, but it's a fact of life.

It makes sense then to choose the messages you wish to send to those around you. You can do this in many ways, but how you dress becomes of utmost importance. By arranging your wardrobe, choosing your colors and your accessories with care you can make a difference in how far you can go in all facets of life. So, everyone will easily grasp the message that is really ***you***, it makes sense to work hard at that first impression you leave.

With this strategic approach to your image, you have an advantage. In your highly competitive society, if you can become noticed as an individual who knows her own style, you are, in a word, ***chic***. Your unique, harmonious, personal message to the world should fit the image you wish to portray in any given situation.

A fashion image is not something you learn overnight. The fashion field professionals; fashion directors of advertising agencies, editors of magazines, and advisors to industry; have not just been born with flair. They cultivated their clothes sense through diligent study and experimentation until they could give good advice to others and use it themselves. You can develop your fashion ability by following these simple methods.

Watch Those Around You

Seeing is believing! If you are serious about learning to improve your image you can do this by observation. Start now to scrutinize those around you and ask yourself the following questions:

- Do their clothes seem plain or fussy?
- Do they fit closely or appear too big as if they belong to someone else?
- Is their choice of colors loud or quiet?
- Do their shoes go with their outfit or are they too plain or fancy?

When you observe them, does the person look neat, their appearance natural or set, or their outfit reek of expensive?

- Do they carry off the clothes well?
- Is the style the height of fashion or do you get the feeling it's their own style?

If you start questioning the styles worn by others and see what it is that appeals or doesn't appeal to you, you can begin to visualize what your fashion ambition is.

Attend Fashion Shows

Whether in department stores, annual showings of the seasons, or a traveling fashion show, you can be sure that what you see at these exhibitions has been carefully orchestrated from head to toe. Fashion shows are carefully organized by a professional stylist or a woman or man known for their chic. The way the clothes are shown, the technique of holding handbags, the accentuating of the outfit with the right jewelry, or the way the model wears the hat, will all give you new clues as to smart ways of wearing what you have or the dress or suit you may be considering.

Attend as many fashion shows as you can and watch not only the styles being shown, but how they are worn and accessorized. Watch how the model carries herself as she walks down the aisle to present the attire. Each piece she is wearing is important to notice and how she moves will play an important part in the way you react to the style.

Go Where Good Clothes Are Worn

Go into some of the finest dress shops and shoe stores. Don't be embarrassed about

not buying but ***do*** try on coats, suits, dresses until you get the feel, first hand, of a fine, beautifully made outfit. And watch the other shoppers; the clothes they wear, their accessories and the styles they are looking for.

Study Fashion Magazines

Read them thoroughly and with a discriminating eye. Watch the details of the fashion, the angle of hats, the slope of shoulders, the length of beads, the shape of earrings, the type of jewelry being worn and shown. Keep an eye on hosiery colors and textures. While you're at it, check out the new and different make up techniques with lipstick, powder. Go a step further and notice the hair styles and the choice made in nail polish. Small changes can total up to new fashion impressions.

Read, look, and think! Ask yourself if what you see is suitable for you and your way of life.

Since you will not be able to afford all the styles that you like, start cutting out pictures of hats, coats, dresses, etc. that you think are fabulous or ones that fit the image you wish to portray. Cut out pictures of clothes that you feel you would like to own and wear. When you look at your scrapbook you need to be critical, but not too critical as you ask yourself the following:

- Would this show off my figure to its best advantage?
- Would this go with other clothes I now own?
- Is this faddish and has a short fashion life?
- Does this look like me?
- Would it fit into the life I lead?
- Would it fit into the life I want to lead?

By asking these questions, you will begin seeing your fashion sense evolve as you limit your choices to add to the scrapbook.

The Basic Wardrobe

A basic wardrobe is hard to define, but necessary if you are to make your clothes work for you. As a guideline, a basic wardrobe should include the following items of clothing:

Casual Coat	Dressy Jumper
Casual Jumper	Jeans
Straight Skirt	Cardigan Sweater
Pleated Skirt	Slacks
Tailored Shirt	T-Shirt
Pullover Sweater	Crop Pants
Tailored Jacket	Shorts
Dress Coat	Jean Jacket

Looking at this list of sixteen items you can begin classifying the items you now have in your closet. This will help you realize your present wardrobe needs. These sixteen basic items combined will allow you to provide for any number of different combinations.

Next you will need to look at your accessories. Again, this is a basic listing that will help you get started in identifying your accessories. The accessories you need are:

Flat shoes	Pumps
Sandals	Dressy heels
Knee socks or ankle socks	Pattern stockings
Sheer stockings	Tote bag
Shoulder bag	Clutch bag
Hat	Scarf
Bracelet	Earring
Necklace	

Considering the above listing you should match items with the outfits you have been able to combine from your wardrobe. Later when you really get into the business of taking the inventory you should find that the accessories complement each other and are usable pieces with your wardrobe to achieve a total look.

Now, let's don't waste money. Make a separate list of each piece of clothing. Skirts on one list, dresses on another list, etc. and note also their colors. You will use the outline of the chart that follows to make your own listing of items. Fill in all the areas as this will be important in analyzing your clothes later on as to what you have, what you will need, colors you don't have, fabrics that are missing, etc. Don't leave a single item off the list, no matter how minor it may seem to you. It may be that one thing that could save you money by updating another more expensive item in your wardrobe.

The "***GOES WITH***" column you will fill out after you have a sense of how to mix and match. This should be filled in after you have read this complete section. Also, you will fill out the "***NEED TO BUY***" column later once you understand your individual wardrobe needs better.

You can make additional copies of the chart if you need to or make your own. You want to be as thorough as possible in doing this inventory assignment.

If you want to, you can start by making note of the items that you found in your closet that fall into the categories on the listing. You can also do this for the accessory listing as well. Remember that you only want to put down the items that you can now wear and use and not ones that need some attention.

You might want to make a separate listing of the items that you wish to keep but aren't ready to be part of your wardrobe at this time. Later, after you have had a chance to do the repairs, you can add them. But you don't have to really do this now. You can wait until you finish the chapter and do it later when you have a better understanding of all that comes into play when you start working with fashions.

I need to mention something at this point. When it comes to jewelry, most women are like pack rats, hanging on to items that serve no purpose. You know what I'm talking about, don't you? It's those earrings that you just had to have or the bracelets or necklaces that you never wear because they don't go with your clothing. As hard as it may be, you must honestly face the fact that not everything you presently own is something that you need or that will work with the total picture you plan to portray. It's best to just let them go.

Clothing LIST

General Categories	Qty	Color(S)						Material	Style	Goes With	Need To Buy
Casual Coat											
Casual Jumper											
Straight Skirt											
Pleated Skirt											
Tailored Shirt											
Pullover Sweater											
Tailored Jacket											
Dress Coat											
Casual Coat											
Dress Coat											
Dressy Jumper											
Cardigan Sweater											
Plaid Slacks											
Solid Slacks											
Dressy Jumper											
Jeans											
Cardigan Sweater											
Slacks											
T-Shirt											
Crop Pants											
Shorts											
Jean Jacket											

Accessory List

General Categories	Qty	Color(S)						Material	Goes With	Need To Buy
Flat Shoes										
Pumps										
Sandals										
Dressy Heels										
Knee Socks/Casual Wear										
Pattern Stockings										
Sheer Stockings										
Tote Bag										
Shoulder Bag										
Clutch Bag										
Hats										
Scarfs										
Bracelets										
Earrings										
Necklace										

Life Style Chart

Once you have an inventory of what you have in your wardrobe and your accessories, you need to think about your life style. Do you work, go to school, play sports, relax at home, enjoy nights on the town, enter pageants, exercise in public places, or need a modeling wardrobe? Whatever you do you will need to consider this in your wardrobe inventory. Make a list of the activities and begin checking your present wardrobe to see if you have what you need to fit your life style. You can set up a chart like the one that follows. Make sure you list all the places you would be able to wear each item of clothing.

Lifestyle Inventory Chart

Item	Color				Wear To	Wear With	Wear To	Wear With

Guidelines Of Fashion

It's time to give you some fashion pointers that will help you in critically looking at your present wardrobe. These points will help you later when you are analyzing your needs or wondering where the items in your inventory list can be best suited for your style of living. These are just guidelines and nothing more. Something to give you some food for thought as you start getting your fashion act together.

- Choose blouses in a variety of styles -- each wearable with 1 or 2 other garments.
- Camisoles are cool in summer; use year-round under blazer or suit; combine with a skirt to create a dressy look.

- Knit Shirts such as T-shirts consider in various collar styles; include sweatshirt and consider stripes.
- Short-sleeved is never as dressy as long-sleeved.
- Tailored suit or dress can be accessorized for a dressier look. You can dress it up or down. Solid neutral color is best.
- Create dress effect by matching color top with a skirt.
- If skirt is straight, allow 1 inch for ease at sides.
- Include solids, stripes, prints and/or plaids in your casual look.
- For a dressy look, solid color, fuller style is most versatile; lightweight fabric is dressier and more flattering.
- Split Skirt is a terrific item for dress, casual or school!
- Fabric weight is most important for maximum wear in suits
- Choose classic design in neutral color for year-round wear and versatility; vary collar and skirt style in additional purchases.
- Item for cooler climates; choose suitable weight.
- Neutral classic works well for cocktail/theater; bright color adds pizazz.

- Suits are nice for travel; combine blazer for a nice look.
- Choose a neutral sweater shade first, and then add color.
- Short-sleeved cardigan can serve as summer jacket. Long-sleeved is indispensable for layering.
- V-neck pullover is most slimming style. Crew-neck is a sporty classic. Turtleneck is wonderful for layering; nice to have in any weight, especially cotton.
- A vest is most flattering in a length that touches hip bone; great for warmth without bulk.
- No skills are required to dress for sport!
- Bathing Suit Cover-up is nice for pool or patio.

Golf Skirt, leotard, tennis dresses, warm-up suit are fun to have, even for the spectator!

the ultimate *skirts* fashion vocabulary

Wardrobe Stretching

Whether you work or go to school you will need to make use of all the tricks of the trade to stretch your wardrobe. Two ideas that have become the mainstay of woman are the blouse and skirt and the jumper. The next most hard-wearing item next to your coat and suit will be a straight dark skirt, preferably black or a soft blue, green, or gray. In winter your skirt should be cut as simply as possible and made up of a good plain wool or broadcloth. In summer it can be of linen or a crease-resistant linen-like fabric. Because you will wear such a skirt so often, you may need to buy one each year.

- The blouse you will wear with your skirts will be the same color but not the same fabric. Here you are talking about the basic blouse. You will of course have other blouses you will wear with it, but your mainstay must be part of your wardrobe.
- The jumper can be worn either informally with sweaters or blouses then quickly changed into a chic cocktail dress when worn on its own with the addition of jewelry.
- These are the basic items that will add versatility to your wardrobe and be able to interchange with other items easily to stretch your wardrobe to limitless looks.

- In putting items together, you need to consider certain points to be sure they work. Some ideas to begin with could be the following:
- A woolen dress worn with a bolero type jacket.
- A button down the front cotton skirt worn with a blouse linked together with a contrasting belt.
- The same skirt worn over a bathing suit for a beach outfit or sun dress.

But there are indeed many ways to connect clothing once you have the basics down. The basics are:

- Coordination of line
- Coordination of fabric textures
- Coordination of colors

Coordination of Lines

Times have changed but the basic rules still can apply of a slim skirt with slim jacket, a fussy blouse with a simple skirt. Your aim for a basic look will be to have an uncluttered look about you. Then, for those special situations you can reverse the trend. Coordination of lines plays an important role in making your clothing work well together.

Coordination of Fabrics

There are no hand-fast rules. In assembling separates try

to avoid the fabrics that are difficult to coordinate. These are gabardines, silk shantungs, linens, and the synthetic fibers such as nylon, rayon, and Dacron. Fabrics that work well together are the following:

- Cotton with cotton-knit jersey
- Velvet or velveteen with wool jersey
- Velvet or velveteen with pure silk taffeta
- Dress woolens with pure silk taffeta or satin
- Angora wool with tweeds
- Shantung with silk jersey
- Corduroy with tweeds
- Flannel with worsted wools
- Wool jersey with tweeds, broadcloth, silks, taffeta, satins, and worsted wools.

Coordination of Color

This takes a full discussion and that will follow next, but basically, color plays a vital part in your wardrobe. Shades like black, white, beige, gray, brown and navy should form the core of your wardrobe. They combine beautifully with each other and provide an excellent background for accessories.

Colors can be used to attract as well as camouflage. Dark colors conceal while light and bright colors reveal. Therefore, you should avoid wearing vivid colors on an area of your body that you don't want to call attention to. Also, the closer a color is worn to your face, the more flattering it should be.

Coloring Your Wardrobe

Your best guide for your most flattering colors is achieved by using colors that work with your skin tone. In the makeup section you determined your skin tone on the key tone chart. This skin tone applies again when choosing the colors that will look best on you. When you know your skin tone, your job is to find special colors that will complement your general coloring. You'll find that once you have your complexion in balance with a flattering foundation, you can wear many more colors than you have ever imagined.

To begin checking out colors, gather together bits of cloth in every shade imaginable. Sit at your mirror in strong daylight. Drape fabrics close to your face and see which shades make your eyes look brighter, your skin softer, and your hair glow. You can instantly see your best colors this way. When you have discovered the best of the lot, experiment with lipsticks. Tiny sample sizes are your best bet. Try them all with the different fabrics, and you're sure to find the winning combinations.

Color can be the magical spark of your wardrobe.

Properly chosen, color can compose you into a harmonious picture from head to toe. But it takes more than color alone to effect the change.

Color works hand in hand with line and proportion to create optical illusions. The optical illusions benefit you by camouflaging your figure and feature faults or psychologically affecting both yourself and those around you. What this means is that what is envisioned is not actually what is seen.

This may seem vague but take a look at the diagrams that follow, and you can begin to understand. The diagrams demonstrate the theory of line, proportion, and color to create optical illusions. After you view the effects, you can get an understanding of the importance of concentrating on line, proportion, and color in the clothes you wear. Then you will go on to first get an understanding of each point so that you can begin to learn how to make line, proportion, and color work for you.

Color works hand in hand with line and proportion and can create optical illusions to camouflage figure and feature faults or psychologically affect both yourself and those around you. Look at the following diagrams that demonstrate the importance of concentrating on line, proportion, and color.

WARDROBE COLOR GUIDE

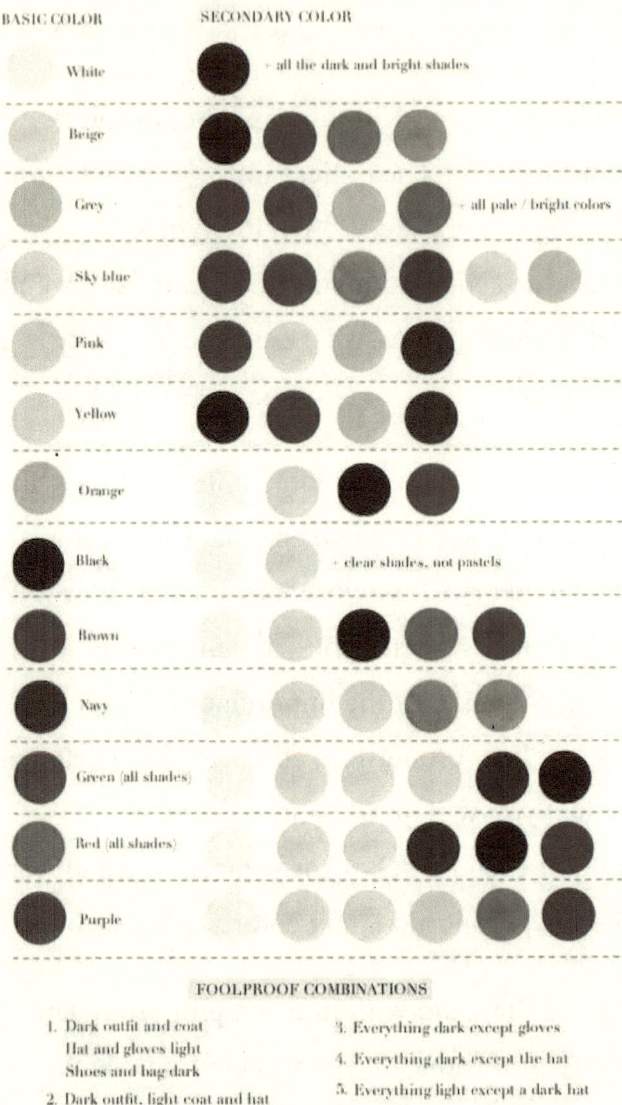

Line Proportion & Color

- These two lines are the same length, but the open

"V" ends seem to extend the line and the close "V" ends seem to shorten the lines.

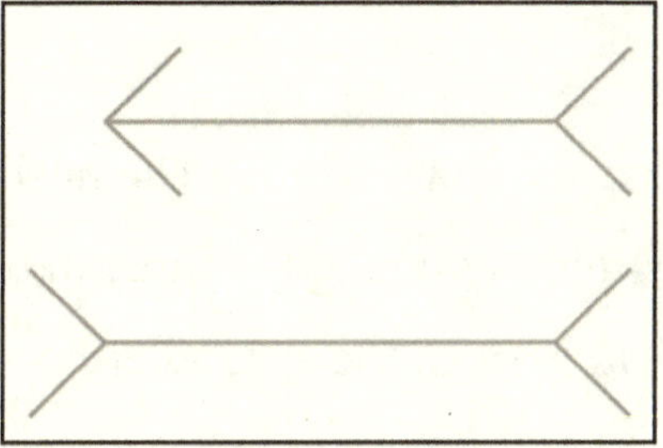

- The two rectangles are the same width. The lines in the first box appear to make the rectangle bulge. The lines are straight.

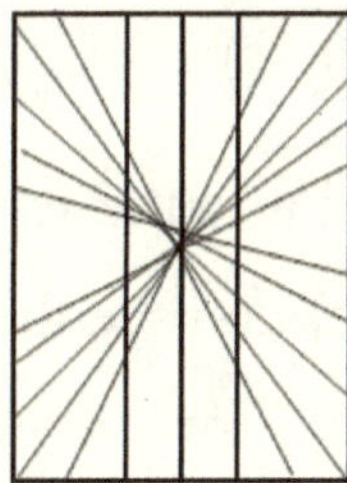

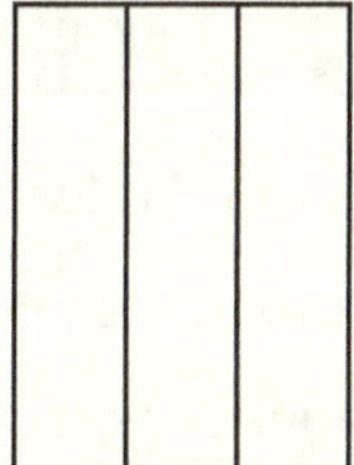

- The line in the center of the first set of three lines is the same length as the center line in the second set.
- The two diamonds are the same width.

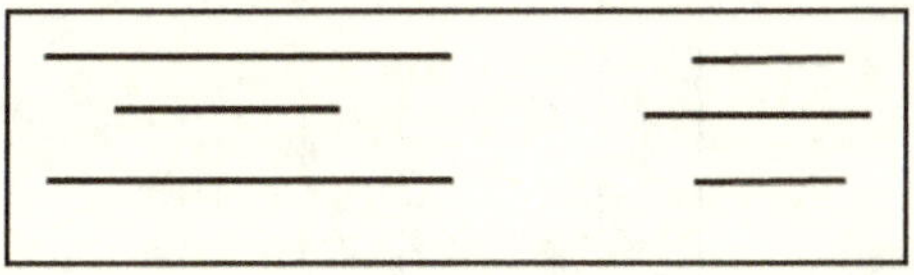

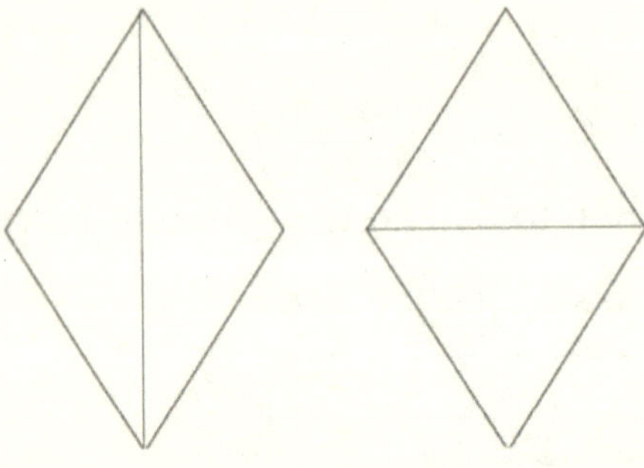

- Both oblongs are the same width. The horizontal lines in the first picture create the illusion of width while the vertical lines in the second create the illusion of length and narrowness.

- Your eye falls on the focal point in the second shape. Without the focal point you see the full rectangle shape. If you have a poor silhouette use a focal point pattern or accessory.

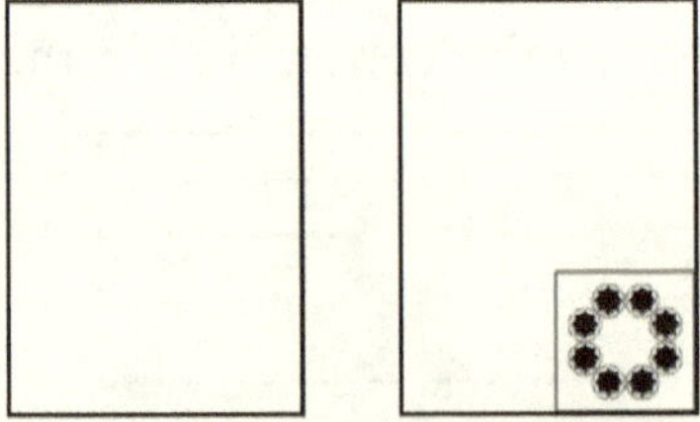

- Proportion camouflages shape. Light top areas grasp the eyes attention and detract from bottom dark areas. Wide hips with narrow shoulders can benefit from this proportion camouflage trick.

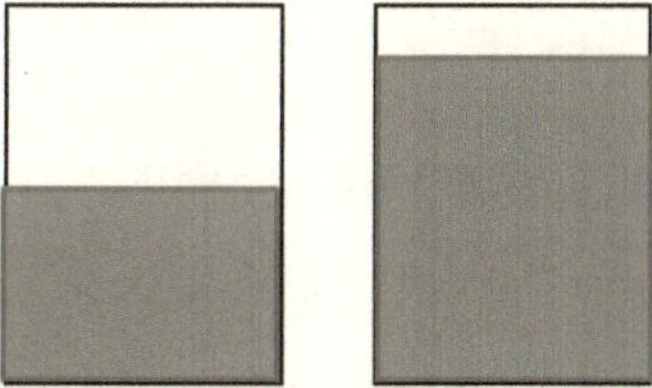

- Dark on either side of light seems to narrow the figure.

The color of your skin, your hair, and your eyes all harmonize in their own unique "color pattern". You can make your "natural colors" harmonize with many other colors when you understand the basic principles for making your selections. First, let's look at how the color of your skin is placed into categories of the seasons. You have probably heard of color analysis, and if so, this will be familiar to you. Your skin color falls into four (4) seasonal color ranges:

- Spring
- Summer

- Autumn
- Winter

When you follow seasonal color ranges your general approach to color selection is greatly enhanced. But to further personalize your image you must deal with all your natural coloring.

You're taking this process a step further by carefully matching your hair, skin, and eye colors with mathematically precise color coordinates. You will create a customized palette, reflecting your own personal coloring system. Your personal color palette should contain tones you can easily match, combine, and coordinate in your makeup and clothing choices. You will know the colors you can wear with anything because they are perfectly you and you can express yourself with complete color confidence.

Basic Facts About Color

Primary Colors

Secondary Colors

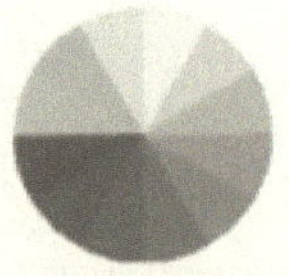
Tertiary Colors

There are six basic colors that you need to be concerned with. These six colors are divided into two groupings of primary and secondary colors.

The three primary colors are red, yellow, and blue. It is these three primary colors that make up the rainbow or spectrum colors.

The three secondary colors are orange, green and violet. You get the three secondary colors by mixing the primary colors as follows:

- Red plus yellow produces orange
- Yellow plus blue produces green
- Blue plus red produces violet

This gives you six "pure" bright colors that you can mix to get intermediate colors such as b*lue-violet, blue-green, yellow-orange, yellow green,* and many other combinations.

In addition to the primary, secondary, and intermediate colors, there are the three neutral colors of *white, black,* and *gray*. The intermediate colors contain none of the primary colors and included in this category are *brown* and *beige* as fashion neutrals because they are versatile enough to be combined with all colors. These five neutral colors of *white, black, gray, brown* and *beige* are known as the workhorses of your wardrobe, or the background colors in clothes selection that can be combined with all other colors to create attractive ensembles.

Color Language

Learning correct color terms is important as you will use them constantly in determining the exact color combinations for your wardrobe. But there are other concerns to deal with, one being color language. Color language includes the following terms:

Hue: This term refers to the name of a "pure" bright primary or secondary color such as red, yellow, blue, orange, green or violet.

Value: This term deals with the lightness or darkness of a hue and is determined by the amount of white it contains or the amount of black. Every hue has high and low values. For example, the hue red shows you a high value of pink which is nearest to white. An example of a low value of red would be maroon which is nearest to black. Both pink and maroon are of the red hue with a variance in the value.

Intensity: Intensity refers to the brightness or the dullness of a color. Intensity is determined by the amount of ray the color contains. The more gray added, the less intense it becomes. Fabric influences intensity. Dull surfaces tend to subdue colors and decrease their intensity. Shiny surfaces reflect the light and therefore increase the intensity. Thus, the intensity of red wool is lower than the intensity of red satin.

Tint: A tint or pastel refers to a hue that has a high value. In other words, a hue to which white has been added would be pint which is a tint or pastel of red.

Shade: A shade refers to a hue that has a low value. Think of maroon which is a shade of red to which black has been added.

This takes a little concentration to understand and grasp. You might want to read this over again before going on. Once you understand the principle, you will be better able to relate to the details that follow.

Color Combinations

The most important fact to be learned about standard color combinations is that any two colors can be combined if the proper shades and tints are selected. On the page that follows you will see a color wheel. As you look at the color wheel, take notice of the key which explains which are primary, secondary, and intermediary.

A standard color wheel puts a picture in your mind that helps in deciphering the importance of knowing the primary, secondary, and intermediary colors that you will work with in coloring your wardrobe.

Color Wheel

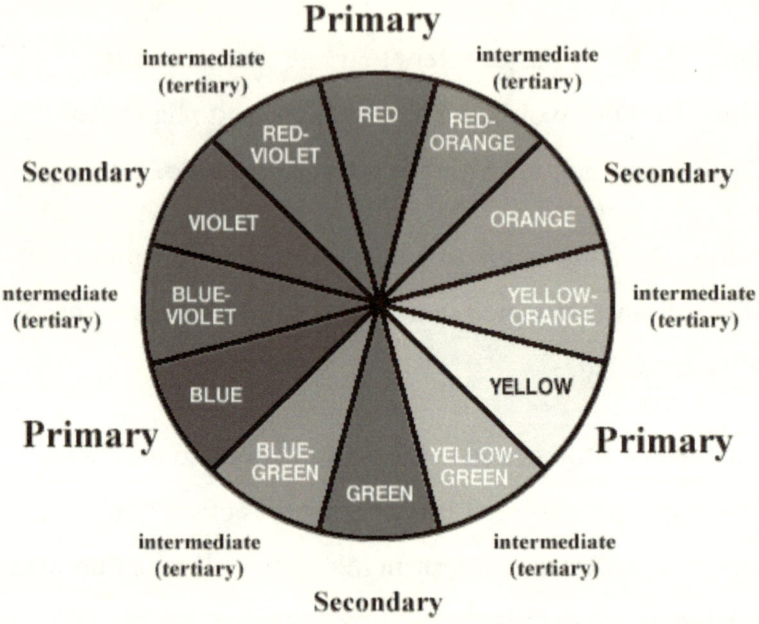

There are five important facts you consider in combining color harmoniously in your wardrobe and they are monochromatic, analogous, triadic, complementary, and split-analogous. You're probably looking at the words with confusion, but once you read the descriptions below, you will better understand the terminologies. Let's look at these terms now.

Monochromatic: A monochromatic combination is made up of only one hue using various intensities and values. For example, a pink wool suit with maroon shoes and a maroon bag is a monochromatic combination. In this example the hue is red, and the tint is pink with the shade being maroon. High intensity is achieved by the shiny surface fabrics and low intensity is achieved by wearing the dull surface fabrics.

Analogous: This is a combination of two hues that are neighbors on the color wheel. For example, blue and green or blue and violet. For best effect they should also vary in value and intensity. An example would be a dull-textured navy-blue suit with a violet satin scarf.

Triadic: This combination is made up of three hues that are an equal distance apart on the color wheel. Take for example, red, blue, and yellow. In your ensemble you should vary the colors in value and intensity. You might choose a dark blue coat, pale yellow straw hat, and trim it with a red velvet band.

Complementary: This is composed of two hues that are directly opposite on the color wheel. For example, red and green, or yellow-green and red-violet. To avoid monotony, they should also vary in value and intensity. You might wear a maroon crepe dress with jade jewelry.

Split-Analogous: A combination of two or more hues separated by only one other hue would be a split-analogous. For example, red and blue, or yellow and blue. Again, these should vary in value and intensity for harmony. You might, for example, choose a pink polished cotton dress and wear it with a navy suede belt and navy suede shoes.

This should help you see that if you vary the colors in value and intensity to eliminate monotony, you can combine any two colors successfully. You will gain more understanding by looking at the fashion color wheel that follows. It will help you begin to associate color with fashion.

When looking at this wheel, read out toward the "parent" hues for shades of the color wheel, and in toward the white of the wheel at the center of the circle for tints. It should all begin to make sense to you now. If not, go back and reread the previous sections before going on.

Fashion Wheel

A TYPICAL
"FASHION" COLOR WHEEL

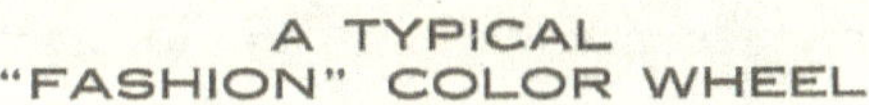

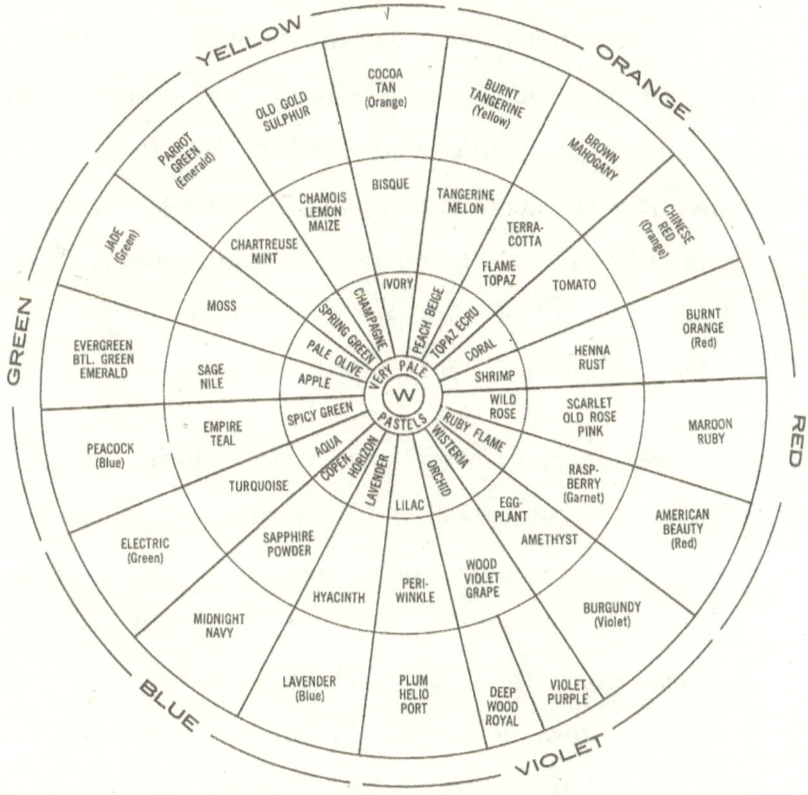

NOTE: Read out toward "parent" hues for shades; read in toward white at center of circle for tints—

Color and Emotional Associations

Colors have psychological effects and you think of them in this sense. Pastels are light-hearted and feminine and associate themselves with Spring. Brilliant hues carry a strong emotional impact of the dramatic and active while dark shades carry a restful, mature, and rich impression. Neutrals give a feeling of depression and can be drab unless they are accentuated with a color or worn in dramatic contrast. That's why the colors you wear can have a tremendous emotional effect not only on you but also on those around you. The reaction of people toward you can vary by your choice of colors. You may find someone is in tune to your way of thinking one day and the next you seem to be on different wave lengths. That's why your choice of colors should reflect not only your "*color personality*", but that of those around you.

When you speak of "*cool*" and "*warm*" colors, the very presence of light can be felt in a warm color. There is warmth on the skin in yellow sunlight. At the opposite end, the lack of light manifests itself in a feeling of coolness or a sense of calm. There is coolness in a breeze that comes from blue water and blue sky, a calmness to gray fog and mist. Much of the earth that is warm and dry is orange, yellow and tan and much that is wet and transparent is blue and green.

You can now understand why red, yellow, and orange are considered to be warm colors, while blue, green, and violet are of the cool family of colors. Both psychologically and visually, warm colors are advancing and energetic. Cool colors are receding and symbolic of repose. Summarized, warm tones bring an object closer and make it appear larger, while cool colors make an object seem further away and smaller.

Blue undertone will give a "*cool cas*t" to all shades, the yellow undertone, and a "*warm cast*". It's a known fact that most people have a definite and natural preference for one or the other of these two undertones, depending on their own personality type, but you need to choose the tone that works best for you. Let's revisit the primary, secondary, and intermediate colors thinking this time in their relation to being warm and cool:

Primary Colors: Red is the bright color of fire that gives a feeling of warmth and excitement. It is a compelling color, splendid, rich, and dignified. If you are an introvert red probably makes you feel uneasy and you may even resent the intrusion of this color around you. Blue is the cool, serene color that suggests peace and remoteness. If you are an extrovert, you may feel indifference to all but the most intense of blues. Yellow is a spring and summer color suggesting warm sunshine. It is a light and cheerful color.

Secondary Colors: Green takes a bit of each feeling of yellow and blue which make up green. It is truly a cool and restful color that will bear much repetition. Violet which is a mixture of red and blue in light tones, pastels, will typify reserve, daintiness, and femininity. In rich, dark shades it is influenced more by the red tones and transmits a warm feeling of dignity and splendor. Orange which results from the mixing of red and yellow is both cheerful and exciting but not to the degree of its parent colors.

Intermediate Colors: All intermediate colors take on, to a lesser degree, the same feelings of their dominant parent colors. You will see aqua as restful and calm, but not to the extent of blue.

Knowing the general feelings of colors, you may want to wear a bright red or yellow on a rainy day to lift your spirits or wear cooler tones on a sunny day to over shadow the warmth. Or if you need to feel self-control, wear a calm color such as blue, blue-green or green to help fight nervousness rather than an exciting or depressing tone.

Your Wardrobe

Flesh, whether it is pinkish, brownish, or yellowish in tone, is always neutral. It is the background color that nature has given you, highlighted by the color of your hair and eyes and your own personal accessories that are in harmony with your skin color. There are many factors to be considered in selecting your personal wardrobe and color will play in important role in your choice. But there is more you need to think about. You need to know which colors do the most for you.

Analyze yourself carefully as you go through this section and think in terms of your personality type, your skin tone, and your hair color. The proper colors for one of your features may conflict with the proper color for another. You will have to decide which features you want to play up and which to play down. Now, let's learn how you should consider colors when it comes to your wardrobe.

Your Personality

Are you vivacious and gay? Then clear colors will express your outgoing nature. You will want colors to correspond with your nature.

Are you dramatic, spectacular? Then you will want to wear brilliant jewel-tone colors and dramatic combinations of neutrals.

Are you shy and retiring? Then don't overdo grayed hues and neutrals for they will merely make you look more mousey. Wear colors of middle value and medium intensity.

Are you feminine and delicate? Soft pastels and light neutrals will frame your fragility. Keep your colors in tune with yourself.

Are you exotic and mysterious? Then you can closely follow the colors for the dramatic woman with emphasis on the rich, warm shades. Contrasts and colors can be subtler for the dramatic type.

Skin Tone

The chart that follows will help you pick colors that will work well with your skin tone. Find your skin tone on the left and look at the choices that are listed for colors that work well with your skin tone and what you should try and avoid.

Skin Tone Chart

Skin Tone	Your Choice	Avoid
Light	Black, Gray, Ivory, Tan, Light Green, Blue Orange, Red, Pink, Lavender	Strong Colors As They Will Tend To Make Your Delicate Coloring More Pallid.
Medium	Mushroom Brown, Navy, Light Gray, Ivory, Tan, Clear Green, Blue-Green, Red, Orange, Pink	Yellow And Colors With Yellow In Them, Such As Yellow-Green. Purple And Black Should Also Be Avoided.
Dark	Black, Warm Brown, Gray, Navy, Ivory, Clear Dark Green, Blue, Red	Colors With Yellow In Them. Also, Purple And Tan.

Next you need to consider the colors that will help to enhance the color of your eyes. On the chart that follows, find your eye color, and then look at the choices that work well with the color of your eyes.

Eye Color Chart

Eye Color	Your Choice
Blue (Gray-Blue, Blue-Green)	Blue Eyes Will Reflect Whatever Color Is Worn. They Can Be Made To Appear Gray, Violet, Or Green When These Colors Are Worn Near The Face. To Accent The Color Of The Eyes Wear The Same Color Near The Face, But Remember That An Intense Blue Will Make Light Blue Eyes Appear Even Lighter.
Green	Green Eyes Are Intensified By Wearing Tones Of Green, Particularly Very Dark Shades. They Will Assume A Blue Cast When Blue And Blue-Green Colors Are Worn. Red Is The Complement Here, Especially Gold-Red Tones.
Brown	Brown Eyes Are Enhanced By Orange Tones, Especially Coral, And Shrimp Tones And Light Beige. Blue And Blue-Green Are Complementary To Brown Eyes.
Gray	Gray Eyes Nearly Always Appear To Have Flecks Of Color In Them. These Flecks May Be Yellow, Gold, Violet, Green Or Red. To Accent The Eyes Apply The Rules You Have Learned To Accent The Color Flecks. If You Want To Stress The Gray, Wear Gray. Wear Gray Near The Face And All Colors Of Low Intensity That Are Grayed.
Violet	Treat These As You Would Blue Eyes, Substituting Violet For Blue, And Yellow In Place Of Orange.
Hazel	Hazel Eyes Also Contain Several Colors Like Gray Eyes. Highlight The Strongest Color And Place Emphasis On Coral And Gold Tones In Your Wardrobe.

There is one more area to consider and that is the shade of your hair. On the chart that follows, find your hair color, and then look at the choices that you should consider and ones you should avoid.

Hair Shade Chart

Hair Shade	Your Choice
Golden Blonde (A Deep Topaz)	Avoid Using Bright, Intense Shades Of Yellow And Orange Unless They Are Used Away From The Hair. Pale Yellows Are Good Because They Intensify And Highlight The Gold In The Hair. Complement Blonde Hair With Violet And Blue Colors, Also Very Dark Shades Of Green, Blue Or Black.
Platinum (Silvery Blonde)	Accent Hair With Clear Cool Colors. Avoid Muddy Browns, Yellow-Orange Tones, And Warm Grays Or Beige.
Ash Blonde (Drab Blonde)	Avoid Bright Colors That Will Make The Hair Appear Even More Drab. Use Pastels And Grayed Ones To Brighten The Hair In Contrast. Gray Is A Becoming Neutral; Also Good Are Soft Greens, Violets And Pinks. Use Bright Colors For Accents.
Medium Brown (Usually With Gold Or Red Highlights)	Accent The Tone Of Your Hair By Repeating The Gold Or Red To Bring Out The Natural High Lights. If Your Hair Is Quite Drab Without Noticeable Highlights, Do Not Wear Brown Of A Richer Tone Than Your Hair. Natural Complements For Brown Hair Are Colors In The Blue, Blue-Green And Blue-Violet Families.
Dark Brown (With Gold Or Red Highlights)	The Same Rules For The Medium Brown Hair Apply Here, But With Additions. With A Rich Brown Shade Of Hair, Wear Bright Colors Of The Blue Family, Also Reds And Yellows. Pastels Are Becoming But Not As Dramatic.
Auburn (Rich, Mahogany Brown)	All Shades Of Green Will Complement Your Hair, Especially Dark, Rich Shades With A Blue Cast. Use Ivory Whites, Black, Warm Beige, Pastel Blue And Green.
Golden Red (Red With Blonde Highlights)	This Color Is Much Lovelier By Wearing Light Yellow-Reds Such As Tea-Rose, Peach And Similar Tones. Avoid Blue-Red Tones. The Same Complement Is Used Here As For The Auburn Hair; Green, Blue-Green And Yellow-Green Colors Such As Chartreuse. Very Dark Browns And Warm Beige Tones Are Good For A Neutral, And Black Is Excellent.
Black	You Can Afford To Take A Lesson From The Latin And Oriental Women Who, With Glossy Black Hair, Wear Such Rich, Bright Colors As Ming Yellow, Jade Green, And Chinese Red. Choose Shades From Any Of The Six Basic Colors Or Their Intermediate Colors, Whichever Are Most Becoming To Your Skin And Eyes. Pastels Will Be A Flattering Accent If Black Hair Is Combined With A Very White Skin.
Gray	Often Gray Hair Has A Brown, Black Or Red Hue. If You Do Not Wish To Accent The Gray, Then Accent The Color In The Hair. Following The Rules Already Given. Gray Hair Can Also Be Effectively Accented By Wearing Grayed Hues In A Darker Shade Than That Of The Hair. Nearly All Colors Look Well With Pure Gray Hair, So They Should Be Chosen To Accent The Skin And Eyes.
White	The Most Effective Accent Here Is The Opposite Neutral Which Is Black. Pastels And Colors Should Be Chosen To Flatter The Skin And Eyes As All Can Be Worn With White Hair.

You will find that the choices will conflict from one chart to the next. This is where you must decide on what features you want to compliment most and make sure that the item you wear is placed strategically so that the features it will most enhance is in direct contact with your color choice.

In general, bright colors will emphasize a skin that is not too clear. A ruddy complexion can be reduced in color intensity by avoiding colors with yellow in them and wearing instead dark gray, greens, blues, reds, mushroom browns, and black.

By now you are getting the idea. To help you further, take swatches of different colors and hold them up against your skin, up closer to your eyes and then look at them as you place the colors next to your hair. Where there some colors that you liked most then others or even some that you found unacceptable for your natural colors? You may have developed a different opinion of color with your new knowledge.

Before you go on, it will be helpful if you take the time to fill in the charts that follow. The information will be useful in helping you as you begin to learn how to look at your wardrobe with a critical eye and having all the information in one location will make it easy for you to refer back as you work your way through the balance of this lesson.

In filling in the information, try to be as accurate as possible and base the information on that recorded on your blueprint and your experience with the colors that you have tested against your skin, your hair, and your eyes. Try not to let your personal preferences play so much of a role they over shadow what you know to be right for you.

Color Graph

QUESTION	RESPONSE
MY SKIN TONE IS	
MY EYES ARE	
MY HAIR COLOR IS	
MY PERSONALITY TYPE IS	
MY BEST COLORS ARE (Fill in shades and tints)	
MY BEST NEUTRALS (*basics*) ARE:	
COMMENTS:	

Fashion-O-Graph

Fill in below your Figure Type, a general description of your problems, and the Camouflage Techniques you will use to disguise faults and play up good features. Insert your response in the second column	
My Figure Type	
GENERAL DESCRIPTION (INSERT MEASUREMENTS):	
Height	
Neck	
Shoulders	
Bust	
Waist	
Hips	
Legs	
MY CORRECT CAMOUFLAGE TECHNIQUES (LINES, PROPORTION, COLOR) ARE:	
General	
Neckline (including jewelry, scarf, etc.)	
Shoulders	
Bodice	
Waistline (including belts, etc.)	
Hemline	
Suit Jackets	
Skirts	
Sleeves (including gloves, jewelry)	
Coat Lines	

Detailing Your Wardrobe

Remember the list of wardrobe items for basics needed in your closet? Let's detail this a little further and include what you have learned about colors:

Background Color

The first color to select is always your "*background*" color/colors for the basic wardrobe items. In making your choices, remember it is possible to change a basic color with the seasons if your budget allows. What you are doing here is just trying to get an idea of what color/colors you will plan for the background of your wardrobe. Once you have made this determination, it's time to think about color for other items in your wardrobe. Look over the following information as you go through your present wardrobe items. If you find you need to make some purchases, write down what it is you need and the color you need to purchase.

Lingerie: Lingerie should include a full slip, half-slip, bra, girdle, and panties. One set should be in white and one set in a basic color. Other colors are optional depending on your wardrobe and your budget.

Shoes: A plain pump for daytime wear in the basic color and in leather or suede for more dressy wear are a necessary part of your wardrobe items. Other colors depend on costumes, your figure, and your budget.

Handbags: Match your first basic shoe in color and in finish. You may want to have your basic handbag in plain broadcloth or a corded bag in a basic color. Additional bags should match shoes in color and in leather or chosen accessory color.

Gloves: A basic in suede or doeskin should be made part of your wardrobe. You should also have a pair of long and short white gloves. It won't hurt to include the same in black.

Dresses: A basic dress should be in a dark or light neutral color. The dress should have a simple style that will easily adapt for day or evening wear by the addition of accessories. A cocktail dress in a favorite color to express your personality is a must. You might also consider a tailored dress that matches the color of your eyes or its complement.

Hats: Select a hat primarily from colors that flatter your skin and hair. If you love to wear hats, you should plan accordingly and have several to choose from in basic colors that will work with your wardrobe.

Jewelry: Precious stones may be chosen from eye color or its complement. If you have costume jewelry chose the items that work as part of the accessory color picture of your wardrobe. Metal jewelry should be chosen to match the highlights of your hair (gold, copper, silver, etc.)

Accessories: Accessories should include belts, scarves, blouses, handkerchiefs, flowers, bows, etc. Select them to accent your outfits. You might want to select pastels to blend with your skin tone, or shades to complement or match your eyes.

Rainwear: Since these items are worn on dull, dreary days, select them in gay, bright colors. Avoid dark and neutral colors unless accented with a bright color.

Evening Wear: Select the color to suit your own taste if not often worn or select a dark neutral that can be changed with colored accents for versatility if you have occasions to wear them often.

Active Sports Clothes: Select an additional basic color for sportswear, shoes, and bags. Follow the same color scheme throughout your sportswear so the items will be interchangeable and provide you with a variety.

Furs: Select furs to complement your hair coloring. Brunettes, gray and white hair should choose black or gray furs. Blondes and redheads need a color to match or blend with their first basic color. Brownettes or dark blondes should choose a shade of brown that is much darker or much lighter than hair, to form a definite contrast and stay away from black or gray.

The Art Of Camouflage

Camouflage is what is known as creating an optical illusion or to put it bluntly, fooling the eye. Camouflage allows you to appear to be one way when you actually are shaped in another way. The rules are that the eye will always follow along the length of a line, and the eye will always be drawn to the lightest color in a color combination. Keep in mind that light colors make an object move forward and appear larger while dark colors make an object move backward and appear smaller. So, in using the colors wisely there are five ways you can adapt them to make your figure seem in perfect proportion:

- Decrease inches with dark colors or increase inches with light colors.
- Add or subtract inches from your height by wearing the right hair style and shoes.
- Choose clothes with lines that will distract the eye away from figure faults.

- Make sure the proportions and silhouette of your clothes are balanced; regardless of a current fashion silhouette or style.
- Add or subtract inches with the fabrics and designs you choose.

Keeping these points in mind, in the game of camouflage your thoughts should be on ***line***, ***proportion***, and ***color***. Here are some tips to help you in applying camouflage techniques.

Hemlines

Every figure has a hem length that will prove most flattering and fashion always provides for a compromise. So, wear your skirts so that they are not conspicuously long or short, but flattering to you. In selecting hemlines, consider the following:

- Irregular hemlines, when they are in vogue, are best worn by medium and tall figures
- Skirts that are short and moderately full can help shorten the too tall figure.
- For thin legs, avoid skirts that are too full or too narrow.
- Beautiful legs are flattered by full or pencil-slim skirts.
- One or more pleats front and back help the too

heavy legs.

Stockings Can Help Camouflage Leg Faults

Just like hemlines can accentuate your legs, your stockings can provide yet another way to camouflage. Look over the following to help you make your choice of stockings.

- Thin legs look best in light stockings;
- Large or heavy legs look best in dark stockings.
- A shiny stocking will make your legs appear larger; a dull finish will diminish their size.
- Thick ankles can be made to appear thinner by wearing darker heels.

Unless you have perfect ankles and legs, avoid fancy heels and fad stockings as you avoid the plague. Remember always, simplicity is the keynote of fashion and this rule applies from your head to your toes.

Now it's time to consider your figure type. Look over the information below that presents figure type descriptions and the information you need in working with your figure when it comes to your choice of wardrobe. Find your figure type and consider the information given below before adding one item to your wardrobe. It will also help you to weed out the items that you now own which will do nothing to enhance your figure type.

PETITE: This figure type is around five feet with tiny bones and delicate proportions. If you wish to play up size, emphasize femininity. You can wear ruffles, laces, and frills. You will find that the empire line also works well on your figure.

To de-emphasize your small size you might consider wearing vertical stripes, tucks, and pleats. These choices will work at lengthening your lines and add height or even width if this is what you want. Also dressing with one color in all your pieces can be most flattering.

Do not use bulky fabrics or large plaids or checks. These will overpower your petite figure. Huge collars, buttons and belts will look overwhelming on your small frame so stay away from them. The same is true of large handbags, hats, belts and two-tone outfits which do not work well with the petite figure.

AVERAGE: This figure is about five feet two to five foot four. Your figure type is usually well proportioned, and you usually find clothes need no altering. You are the lucky one. You are free to follow your own style preference. By experimenting you will find the most flattering silhouettes and colors can be those that are most comfortable to wear and suit your personality best.

As a guide, if your tummy and thighs are heavy, tight sheath lines can look wrong. If your waist is large, try to avoid full or pleated skirts. If your arms are too thin or too heavy it's best to avoid a sleeveless look. And don't wear turtlenecks if you have a full bust.

WILLOWY: You are what is considered tall and thin. Your fashion choice is to cut those long lines. Contrasting colors in tops and skirts is a good alternative for your figure. Bright prints, horizontal stripes, dresses with some waistline emphasis will also prove flattering. High necklines and soft collars can help disguise your thinness.

You should stay away from vertical strips which will only emphasize your long lines and one-color look will tend to do the same. If your arms are extra thin, avoid sleeveless dresses. V necklines add length so do not wear them. You will find that dark tones, especially black, are not a flattering choice.

CURVY: You are somewhere between average or petite in height with soft, feminine lines, or even pleasantly plump.

Your fashion goal is to try to lengthen your line. A good solution is a one-color look. Dresses and sheaths are especially becoming to your figure type. Try to keep the lines smooth through your waistline. Flared or A-line skirts are excellent.

Do not wear horizontal stripes or bright surface fabrics. Bold patterns are also taboo for a curvy figure. Skirts and tops are not a good choice for you. Neither are fullness in skirts, gathers or pleats at the waistline as they will be too bulky. You should also avoid wide belts.

GODDESS: You are tall with large bones and round curves. You haunt the tall girl shops. Your ideal fashion look is similar to the curvy and tall figures combined. That means you can wear two piece looks well and with your height you can carry a more dramatic look. You will also find you are well suited for vertical stripes and definite waistlines.

If your figure tends to be well padded, follow the same don'ts as the curvy figure. Fullness in skirt, gathers and pleats at the waistline will create bulky looks that will be unflattering. Horizontal stripes and bright surfaces should be eliminated from your wardrobe as they will do nothing for your figure type.

CARING FOR YOUR CLOTHES

Now that you have spent so much time in purchasing the clothes, you want to be able to care for them properly so that they will have a long life.

The first step is to look at your closet. How is your clothes closet? Is it neat and well organized or in shambles? If it is, why not take the time now to organize it before putting your clothes back. If you have already placed the clothes you have away, let's get it organized. Empty your closet completely and dust and wash the shelves. Look over the items and make a list of clothing bags and storage boxes that might help you in organizing your clothes. A clothing bag for jackets, one for skirts, and another for short coats will help you get your clothes in order. You might want to investigate putting in one of the closet organizers that can make your closet seem much bigger.

Consider on the shelf putting in storage boxes or plastic see-through units that will be easy to access. A three-drawer dresser for lingerie and other items will also be helpful. You have your clothes out so check what you have and plan what you will need to help organize these items in your closet. Belt racks, shoe boxes, hooks, all these items can help organize your closet and use all available space wisely without jamming up your items.

While you're at it, why not again check over each piece of clothing for mending, cleaning, pressing, etc. And take care of this before placing the items back in your neatly arranged closet. Your clothes should be in perfect condition, with no stains, missing buttons, rips, etc. Your shoes should be polished, heels in good repair, soles not worn down, etc. Once the items of your wardrobe are in tip top shape, then, and only then put them into your "*tip top*" closet arrangement.

Get into the habit of getting out your clothes to be worn the next day, the evening before. Don't make haphazard, last minute decisions on what to wear. You have spent a lot of time in learning how to dress, so don't let it fall by the wayside because you don't have time to spend finding just the right items of clothing.

Finally, take care of all your clothing properly. If an article of clothing needs to be dry cleaned, dry clean it. If it needs polishing, polish it. If it is washable, make sure it is washed before it stains. No matter how careful you are in putting your wardrobe together it will not work if the items of your fashion coordination are not in perfect condition.

LESSON 17:
VOICE & CONVERSATION

Have you ever stopped to think how many hours a day you spend talking with people? Every hour of every day you are revealing yourself to others through conversation. When you communicate it is not only what you say, but how you say it that goes into the message you convey. You may be exquisitely groomed and artfully made up but just a single sentence from your lips in a nasal twang, or a high whining tone can completely destroy the message your appearance should suggest. If you see people looking at you with curiosity as you speak, don't dismay. You can correct your speech by expending a bit of time and energy in correcting your voice and speech problems.

Hearing Your Voice

First you need to hear your voice to determine what you need to correct. The first step is to determine if your problem is a voice fault or a speech fault. You may find that you have some of both. In voice, you will be determining which best describes the sound of your voice:

- Low-pitched

- High-pitched
- Loud Nasal
- Soft Breathy
- Monotonous

Next you will be concentrating on your speech and determine if you practice any of the following faults:

- Mumbling
- Mispronunciations
- Adding syllables
- Omitting syllables
- Slurring
- Slang
- Clichés

All of this you can correct, but you won't know what to work on until you hear yourself speak. So, how to you do this? Well, this can be accomplished in either of two ways.

Corner Method

Stand facing directly into a corner of a quiet room. Take both your hands and place them behind your ears. Speak into the corner, using it as a sounding board. You should be able to hear your voice. The problem with this method is you need to repeatedly go to the corner and keep checking as you try to identify the areas for correction, but it does work.

Of course, today with tape recorders at reasonable prices, it makes it much easier to hear your voice.

Tape Recording

The best method of course is to tape your voice. When you hear your voice played back you are better able to identify any mechanical faults in speech. So, get out your tape recorder and start a conversation with yourself using the following instructions:

- You should talk naturally and not write a rehearsed speech.
- As you talk into the tape recorder, try not to think about anything but putting words on the tape. You are not correcting your voice now. Instead, you are putting words and sentences on the tape, so you can hear how you naturally speak.
- To give you plenty to work with, try and talk randomly for at least five minutes. Remember, it's not what you say, but how you're saying it that matters so don't worry if it doesn't make sense.

When you have completed this exercise, it's time to listen to your voice and the words. Play the tape back as you pay close attention to the tone of your voice and how you pronounce the words. Now turn the tape off and look over the following list of voice and speech faults. Voice Faults

FAULT	DESCRIPTION
Low-pitched	throaty
High-pitched	shrill, squeaky, nagging or whining
Loud	dominating or bossy
Too nasal	twangy
Soft	shy, timid, self-conscious
Too breathy	panting, gasping between words
Monotonous	too even a rate or pitch

Speech Faults

FAULT
Mumbling words
Mispronunciation of words
Adding sounds and syllables to words
Omitting syllables from words
Slurring words together
Slang
Clichés

Did you hear any of these in the play back? Play the tape again and look at the list above as you try and determine the ones that describe your voice. Play it again as you pay close attention to the pitch. Keep playing the tape until you have noted all the areas of faulty voice and speech habits that you hear on the recording of your voice.

Take your time as you go through this exercise as you don't want to miss anything. You are going to learn how to correct these faults so be critical and don't worry if you find there are several areas where you have problems in speech.

You should now have a good idea of the faults that are part of your speech. Just to be sure, replay the tape again as you look over the charts above and then begin recording your findings on the charts below. Once you have done this, it will be time to go on. But a word of caution: Don't rush through this step! This is a lesson in learning how you speak, and you want to be the expert on knowing what it is you do wrong.

My Voice Errors

My Speech Errors

The Starting Point

Before you can begin to correct these errors, you have to learn how to listen. Listening is an art. You should start listening to not only how you sound, but how others sound around you. Hearing others speak will fine tune your ability to identify not only improper speech and voice faults, but the sound of the voice when speaking correctly. Start to listen with attention, alertness and with interest to yourself and others. You won't be able to *'sound'* what you cannot hear.

Your first assignment: The best way to go about this is to encourage conversation. Talk with your friends and family and listen closely to the words they say, how they say it, and critically evaluate their voice. Do this for at least one week.

Your second assignment: Start a conversation with an acquaintance or someone who you find you enjoy talking with. Analyze the sound of their voice, the tones they use and the words that come from their mouth. Try and determine what it is that you like about their voice or dislike and take notes. Once you have completed this phase, there is one more.

Your third assignment: Listen to people talk on the radio and television. Listen closely to the sound of their voice. Ask yourself if you can discover what they feel just by the way they speak. Try and ascertain whether you like the way they talk or not. Discover what it is that forms your opinion. Is it the tone of their voice, or the words they use?

Once you have completed this exercise you are ready to start working on your voice and conversation. All that you are about to learn will make sense now that you understand the effect that voice and speech faults can have on the spoken word. After listening closely to people as they speak, you can determine what you like and dislike about the way they use their voice in conversations. So, when you're ready, let's begin to make you a wonderful speaker.

Breathing

At the base of proper voice control is breathing. I refer to proper breathing from the diaphragm rather than from the chest area. Breathing for voice requires conscious effort to establish the habit of a reserve supply of breath to support the tone through a period of speaking. To learn diaphragm breathing so that it becomes a conscious process, different from chest breathing, practice the following:

Stand in front of a mirror and watch your chest as you take several slow breaths. Does your chest rise and fall? If so, you are normally a chest breather.

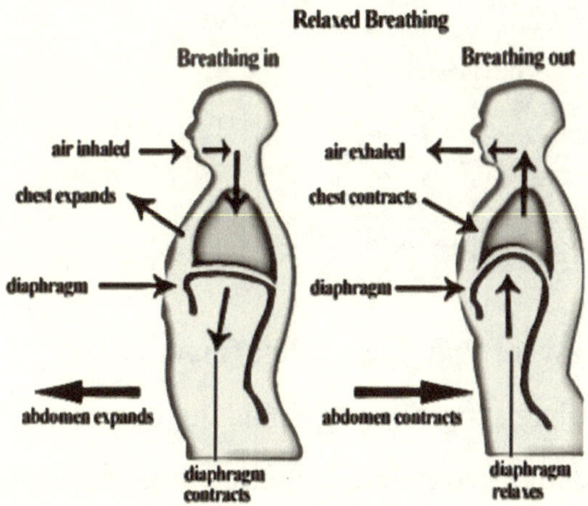

Now lie down on the floor and place your hands on your diaphragm which is located just over the lower rib cage. Have your index fingers touching.

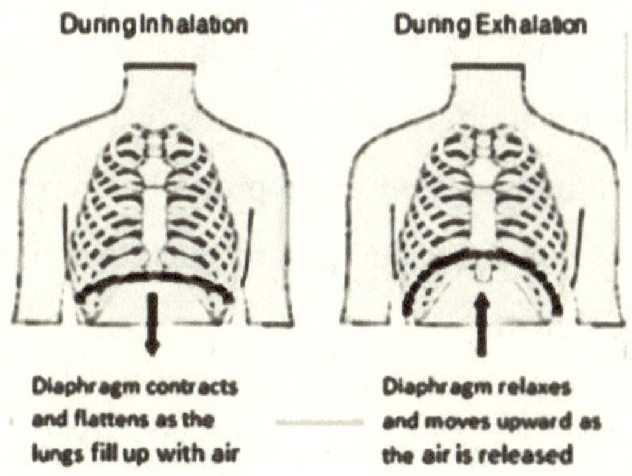

Relax completely and try not to think of how you are breathing with your conscious mind.

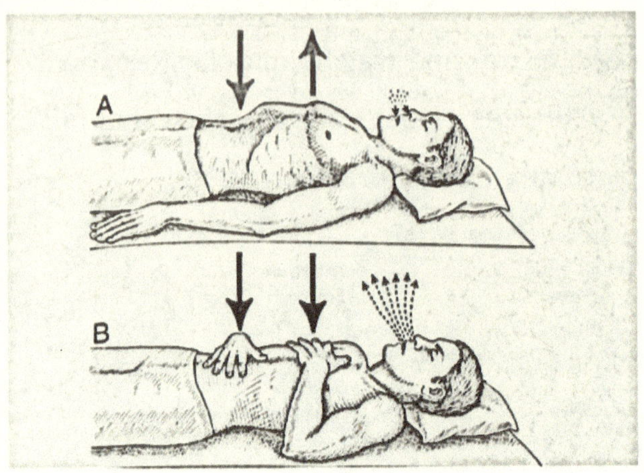

You will become aware that your index fingers are moving apart then back together again as the big diaphragm muscle takes over and breathe correctly for you.

This is the way nature intended for you to breathe always, not just when you are asleep. Did you find you were a chest breather and not a diaphragm breather? Were you able to correct this? If not, don't worry, it takes exercise to master diaphragm breathing. The exercises that follow will help you in learning how to breathe properly from the diaphragm. Take your time and perfect each exercise before going on to the next.

Exercise 1: Lying on your back with your hands over your diaphragm, take a deep breath; hold; let it go. Make sure your throat is relaxed and not closed while you hold your breath. Repeat 10 times.

Exercise 2: Sit in a chair in your good posture position of hips back, chest high. Make sure you're comfortable with the position before you begin then place your hands over the diaphragm to feel its action. Breathe in and out until the diaphragm breathing pattern is established. Now take a deep breath; hold; exhale. Repeat 10 times. Next inhale; hold; and whisper as you exhale. Repeat 10 times. Again, inhale; hold; and try to blow out an imaginary candle as you exhale, but again without using effort. Repeat 10 times. Before you go on, get that tape recorder. Record yourself as you work through the following exercises. When you complete an exercise, play back the tape so you can hear your voice. If you're satisfied with the results, go on. If not, redo the exercise and tape it again. Continue until you are sure you are doing each one right and you like the results.

Exercise 3: Sing the diatonic scale as it appears below.

You will begin at the bottom and step your voice up until you reach the last "Do"

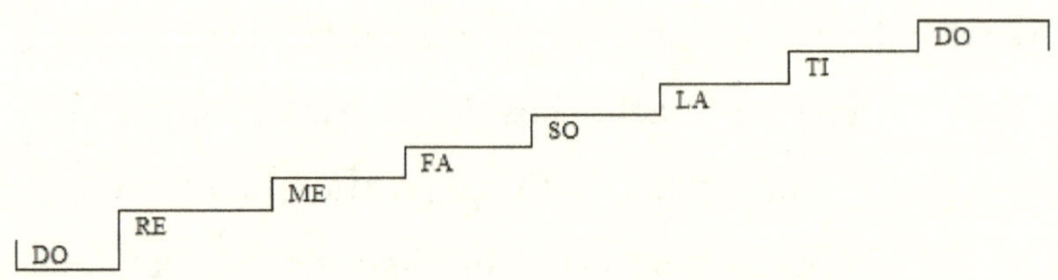

Sound the vowel ***a*** as in father on a rising inflection (*like steps up a scale*). Let it float out on your exhaling breath. Be careful that you do not tighten either your diaphragm or upper chest. You should inhale for the sound, make the sound, and then relax. Repeat 10 times.

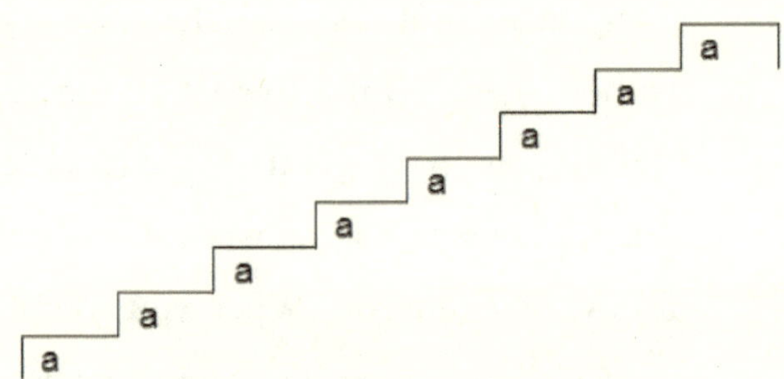

After locating the proper breathing center of the diaphragm, the next step is to learn to retain enough breath to make a full sustained tone. You must also take care not to take too much breath at one time. It is better to fill your lungs frequently than to try to hold more breath at one time. Are you feeling more natural as you breathe? Continue with the following exercises.

Exercise 4: Sit as before with your hands placed over your diaphragm. Take a breath and hold it. This time as you breathe out count aloud from one to ten. Take a new breath with each number and use rising inflection as you count, covering at least one octave of the scale. Think of the way you say the musical scale. Your voice seems to be climbing upstairs with each sound. This is raising inflection. Don't forget to inhale for the sound, make the sound and then relax.

Repeat the exercise using downward inflection. At first you may find it difficult not to sing the numbers but practice until you are able to speak each number in a rising and descending inflection. Repeat this exercise 10 times.

Exercise 5: Now stand up. Move about for the following while keeping your hands over your diaphragm. As you did before, inhale for the sound, make the sound, then relax.

Whisper	Repeat 5 times
Blow out a candle	Repeat 5 times
Pant	Repeat 5 times
Sigh	Repeat 5 times
Yawn	Repeat 5 times
Laugh like this Use three different pitches	ha-ha-ha! Ho-ho-ho! Repeat 5 times

Rate And Pitch Variance

To avoid a monotony in your speech, you should acquire a variety in both the rate in which you speak, and, in the pitches, you use when speaking. Rate reflects the meaning of what you are saying, and the pitch variance will make your speech more interesting.

When you speak rapidly you are expressing joy, excitement, eagerness, or anger. When you speak slowly you are expressing sorrow, awe, wonder, reverence, dignity, or a serious thought.

Try reading the following lines at a very rapid pace, then at a very slow pace. See how much more exciting the rapid pace makes the lines sound?

Hats off!

Along the street there comes

A blare of bugles, a ruffle of drums,

A flash of color beneath the sky:

Hats off!

The flag is passing by!......

Henry Holcomb Bennett, The Flag Goes By

Notice how much variety of pitch you achieved in reading rapidly. Now read the following lines.

My candle burns at both ends;

It will not last the night;

But ah, my foes, and oh, my friends--

It gives a lovely light!

Edna St. Vincent Millay

Now read both passages again, varying the pitch from word to word, and from phase to phrase. At first your voice may sound unnatural to you at a lower or higher pitch then you are used to. With practice though you will begin to get a much better understanding of what you are reading by changing your pitch as your voice begins to reflect the meaning of what the words are saying.

The following exercises will give you practice in hearing yourself speak at different pitch levels. These practices will help you obtain a variety of pitches in your speech.

The object is to go up and down the scale in spoken syllables. Do not sing the sounds but speak the sounds as you inhale for the sound, make the sound, and then relax. Let's begin.

EXERCISE 6: Count from one to eight then back to one on ascending then descending pitch levels. Repeat 10 times.

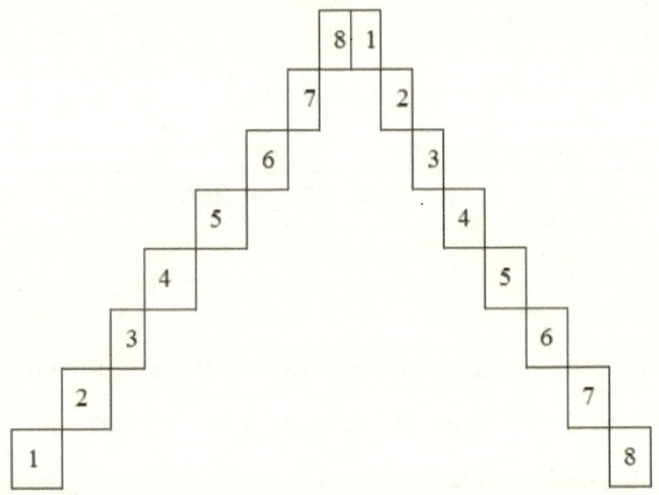

EXERCISE 7: Speaking the sound lightly, and using the syllable ***la,*** repeat the following in ascending and descending pitch patterns. Repeat 10 times.

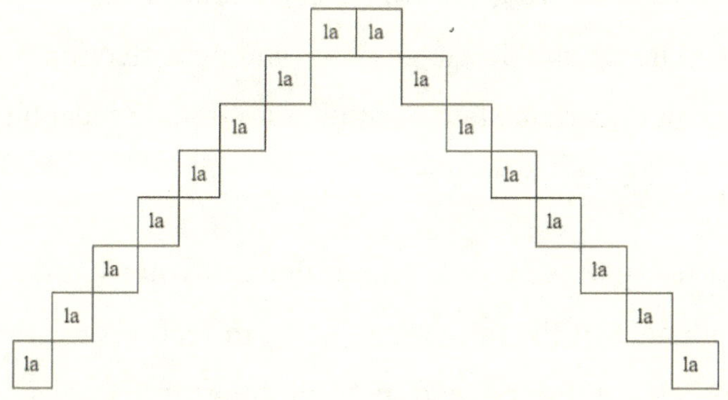

Inflection

Inflection is the act of change in pitch or loudness of the, voice when speaking. Variety in inflection usually indicates a variety in meaning of the spoken word or words. It's time to practice inflection. You should inhale for the sound, make the sound, and then relax.

Exercise 8: Read the following sentence:

"Where are you going?"

- Read it and this time stress the word ***Where***.
- Read it and this time stress the word ***Are***.
- Read it and this time stress the word ***You.***
- Read it and this time stress the word ***Going***.

Can you hear the four different meanings by the words you are stressing? You use a rising inflection (*an upward glide to your voice*) to ask a question. You use a falling inflection (*downward glide*) to reflect a completed thought. The up and down, or down and up inflection indicates an uncertain state of mind, or a double meaning such as used in satire or sarcasm.

Whether using a rising or falling inflection you should vary the length of the inflection. Long inflections express sincerity, clear thinking, and dignity. Short inflections generally reflect a scatterbrain who is incapable of expressing any clear thought. Therefore, when you read or express an important point, you should raise the voice. Raising the voice is far better than shouting, don't you think?

Exercise 9: To see how true this is, read the following memorable sentence from the inaugural address of John Fitzgerald Kennedy:

"And so, my fellow Americans, ask not what your country can do for you--ask what you can do for your country."

Voice Quality

The purity of tone of your voice is the quality of your voice and is dependent upon two things: mechanical and emotional quality.

- Mechanical faults consist of breathy, throaty, nasal tones and huskiness in the voice. You have already practiced exercises to control breathing which helps a lot in limiting the breathy and tones, but you still need work. First, let's understand what causes the mechanical faults.
- Throaty qualities usually result from the constriction and tenseness in the throat and muscles controlling the back of the tongue.
- Nasal tones come from a relaxed soft palate which allows too much breath to pass through the nose in speaking.
- Huskiness is usually caused by forcing the tone until the vocal cords are strained. This is best cured by complete rest.

Let's work on those throaty and nasal tones.

Throaty

The following exercises are to help relax the throat and back tongue muscles and to learn to focus tone forward.

Exercise 10: Practice yawning in front of a mirror until you get the feeling of your tongue being pressed at the back and the feel of your throat fully open. Once you have felt and seen this you can go on to try to depress your tongue and keep your throat open without yawning. When you can do this easily you are ready for sound.

Exercise 11: With your throat open, sound each of the following vowels in turn. Make sure that your lips do their part and the muscles of the larynx are relaxed. Repeat each vowel sound 10 times.

a as in part

a as in all

o as in old

oo as in book

u as in rule

Exercise 12: Again, with your throat open, sound the "***oo***" as in "*book*" and gradually let it merge into the "***o***" sound as i*n* "old" using the same breath. Repeat 10 times.

You should now be ready to learn how to control the placement of the tone. This requires practice as well. If you're feeling strained, stop and relax before you go on. Working on your speech can be taxing. When you're ready, you can begin.

Exercise 13: Now, with the throat open, sound the "***u***" as in "*rule*". Let it merge on the same breath with the "***o***" as in "old" and then the "***a***" as in "*part*". Repeat 10 times.

Now let's go on to learn how to exercise for correct tone placement.

Exercise 16: Pronounce the "***o***" as in "*old*" in such a way that it seems to come from way back in the throat and comes out muffled. Now round your lips and just think the sound of "***o***" through this round opening.

Next make a circle of your thumb and forefinger, hold about six inches in front of your mouth and try to place this same "***o***" sound through this circle. If you are doing this correctly, the vowel will take on a clearer and more brilliant tone.

Exercise 14: Repeat each of the following 10 times, using different pitch levels.

mee mee mee mo mo mo

mee mee mee maw maw maw

mee mee mee moo moo moo

mee mee mee maw maw maw moo moo moo

Nasal Tones

There are three prominent nasal sounds and they are "***m***", "***n***", and "***ng***". For these three sounds, the velum (*soft palate at the back of your mouth which controls passage of breath into your nose and throat*) should be relaxed and wide open. It should be loosely closed but not tense when sounding the vowels and it should be tightly closed for sounding such consonants as "***b***" or "***p***". You can control a nasal tone if you learn to control the opening and closing of the velum. Here are some exercises to help you learn this control.

Exercise 15: Hum the nasal sound "***m***" until you feel your lips tingle. Try it on one pitch then another until you make it sing. Now sound the "***m***" on a middle pitch and quickly change the "***m***" to the velum closed formation of "***b***". Repeat until you are aware of the open action for "***m***" and the closed action for "***b***".

Exercise 16: Repeat the same as above with "***n***".

Changing this time to the sound of the closed velum "***d***". Repeat 10 times.

Exercise 17: Repeat with "***ng***" then change to the sound of the closed velum "***g***". Repeat 10 times.

Jaw, Lips, And Tongue

As you guessed from the start the jaw, lips and tongue play a major role in speaking. Relaxing and developing the flexibility of the jaw, lips and tongue is important both in the formation of sounds as well as the production of easy flowing tones. Let's do some exercises for these areas to help improve your tonal sounds.

You'll begin with lip exercise.

Exercise 18: On a singing note, pronounce ***pa-pi-pi-pa*** on at least three different pitches. Repeat 3 times each, for a total of 9 times.

Exercise 19: Do the same for *ma-mi-mi-ma.*

Exercise 20: Do the same with ***oo-e e-oo oo-e e-oo***. Exaggerate the lip action by rounding and stretching the lips.

Exercise 21: Combine back of tongue and lips with ***ka-pa-ka-pa*** first on a singing note, then on speech notes. Repeat 10 times.

Exercise 22: Do the same with ***ga-ma-ga-ma***. Repeat 10 times.

If you were successful with the lip exercises, let's begin the jaw exercises.

Exercise 23: Form a tight circle with your lips and say "***oo***". Now drop your jaw as far as you can and say "ah". Now alternate the "***oo***" and the "***a***h" as fast as you can. Repeat 10 times.

Exercise 24: Drop your jaw open and sound these syllables, first on one pitch, then change to another. Repeat 10 times.

fa-fi-fi -- fa-fi-fi -- fa fa fa

Exercise 25: Drop the jaw open and say "***ah***". Now lift the jaw and say "***ee***". Now alternate "ah" and "***e***e" as fast as you can. Repeat 10 times.

Exercise 26: Try and combine jaw, tongue, and lips as you practice the following. Repeat each 10 times.

fa-la-fa-la

Alpha-Beta-Gamma-Delta

Were you able to do it? If not, try again, and then let's do some tongue exercises.

Exercise 27: Drop the jaw open and do not move it. Let your tongue do all the work here. Now pronounce these syllables on one pitch, and then change to another. Repeat 10 times.

ga-gi-gi -- ga-gi-gi -- ga-ga-ga

Exercise 28: Do the same with the following. Repeat 10 times.

la-li-li -- la-li-li -- la-la-la

Exercise 29: Do the same with the following. Repeat 10 times.

ta-ti-ti- -- ta-ti-ti- -- ta-ta-ta

Now take a deep breath then exhale slowly as you trill the letter "***r***" on your tongue. Repeat 10 times.

Trilling is the rapid reiteration of the same tone by vibration of one speech organ against another--in this case the tip of the tongue against the teeth ridge.

Exercise 30: For additional practice in exercising the flexibility of the lips, jaw and tongue repeat the following tongue twisters. Tongue twisters have been recommended for curing everything from hiccups, lisps, and other speech defects. Try and not feel silly as you repeat the tongue twisters. Just keep telling yourself they will help increase your ability to speak properly.

- She sells sea shells beside the seashore.
- Peter Piper picked a peck of pickled peppers.
- The sixth sheik's sixth sheep's sick.
- How much wood would a woodchuck chuck if a woodchuck could chuck wood

Correcting Careless Speech Habits

Careless speech habits are apparent when you say *yuh*, or *ya*, when what you mean is **you**. Or you may find that you say *j-ever* for **did you ever** or *j-eat* for **did you eat**. This is a case of careless speech errors. Now, let's see if you notice this. Play back your recordings. How do you sound? Are you beginning to hear improvements?

As you have been doing, you will record as you say the following sentences slowly, then increase your rate until you are saying each one at a very fast pace. Try to depict any careless speech habits as you go along by listening carefully to yourself.

Exercise 31: Repeat the following sentences.

- Did you have a good time?
- When did you see her last?
- What did you do last night?
- Did you ever go up in an airplane?
- Did you know?
- Won't you come in?
- Did you get it?
- Did you ever pay him?
- Give me a little ice cream.

If you noticed any errors here, continue saying these slow at first and then faster until you have each of them mastered with no careless speech.

Enunciation

Enunciation is no more than pronouncing your words with distinction. You will have blurred speech along with incorrect sounds that lead to mispronunciation if you are lazy in the use of your lips, lower jaw, and your tongue. You have learned exercises for strengthening these areas, so you should be in good shape for the following exercises. Along with this the mispronunciation of especially two of your vowels ("***u***" and "***o***") can lead to problems in speech. The long ***u*** sound that you hear in the word "*music*" is a combination of the letter ***y*** and the double ***o***.

Exercise 32 To eliminate getting the long mixed up with the sound of the double ***o*** read these words from left to right:

LONG U	LONG DOUBLE O
due	do
hue	who
moot	mute
beauty	booty
feud	food
tutor	tooter

Concentrate on correcting any mispronunciations that you have made in the past to eliminate them happening in the future. You should be sure that the short double ***o*** as in "*moon*" and long double ***o*** sounds as in "*cook*" or the ***ng*** sound in "*saying*" are being properly pronounced. For instance, you should hear "**saying**" and not "*sayin*" or "**bakery**" and not "*bakry*".

This will be up to you to work on since it would take too much time to cover all the problem words falling in this area. It might be helpful to again listen to others as they speak as it will help you realize the importance of correcting these mispronunciations-pronunciations.

Playing back your take will prove beneficial too.

Slang And Clichés

The best way to eliminate slang and clichés from your speech is to become conscious of them. You should now be an avid listener of your voice from hearing it so much. So, start now to listen to what you say. Is your conversation made up of slang and clichés? You should start to listen for these in your speech. The best way to handle removing them is at the time you use them. From here on out, each time you talk to someone and hear yourself using slang or clichés, stop and excuse yourself and then repeat the sentence correctly. If you stop and think, you may find you don't have to go through the embarrassment of repeating yourself to the listener.

Just as important is trying to correct the quality of your voice. Reading aloud will help immensely toward correcting your emotional quality of voice. When you read aloud you can hear how your voice reflects the tone of the story and if you do this at least 15 minutes you will begin to automatically express the feeling of the words in your voice. This will aid in helping you think clearer and thus improve your speech. With little effort you will find new words cropping into your conversation that will help to express your opinions better. And finally, you will be exercising your mind every time you read aloud. This will lead to improvement in your level of conversation which is the next area you will cover.

Conversation

Conversation is your way of communicating with friends, family, and people that you meet. Having confidence in your appearance is only half the battle. You develop total confidence and ease by also knowing that you can mingle and converse intelligently with friends and strangers alike.

It is said that conversation is a lost art that people aren't listening well enough to actively participate and keep a good conversation flowing. It's sad because not only is conversation necessary for communication, but it can also be entertaining as ideas whirl around a room and participants express their opinions in their own words. The mere act of two or more people having the opportunity to express themselves is one of the most satisfying experiences in life.

Is it a lost art? Well you are going to revive it by learning the essentials of being a good conversationalist. The essentials are that you must think of yourself as both a hostess and a guest and you must be prepared to do the following:

You follow the same essentials when you are talking on a school level at meetings or in general conversation with two or more people.

Assume Your Conversational Responsibilities

If you are the hostess, it will be your responsibility to arrange introductions for individuals with similar interest or taste. You will need to keep your eyes open for stragglers and help them mingle with the guest by performing the introduction and pointing out a similarity in interests. It may also stimulate the conversations if you maneuver guests from one group to another.

If you are a guest, you can help the hostess by listening carefully to the conversations and develop your own knowledge base for circulating between the groups. It will also be helpful to try and draw a shy person into conversation or help a dull conversationalists by "*sprucing up*" the words with your own interpretations. Mingle with the group and listen for clues from the conversations around you to help you approach different people.

Be Able to Open Conversations with Ease

Opening conversations is easy. You can start by introducing yourself. This automatically leads to a response from the person you approach. After that you can use small talk to help break the ice. Talking about the weather is a permissible starting point, or asking about their spouse, friends, interests, etc. will help in getting the conversation rolling.

Have Something Interesting or Important to Say

Once the conversation has begun, have something interesting or important to share with the individual. You may ask their opinion on a world event but remember to avoid politics or religion. Or maybe you have just read or begun reading a best seller. You might try presenting a discussion on the book or the author. Whatever you choose, remember it will be your enthusiasm that will make the conversation interesting. If you are knowledgeable and interested in the subject, it will reflect in your voice.

Once you have the conversation going, know when to stop and steer the conversation elsewhere or allow someone else a chance to broach another subject. You don't want to bore the listeners or "*hog*" the conversation.

Development a Creative Listening Attitude

You'll never learn anything if you do all the talking. Give the other person a chance to add to the conversation and listen with an open ear for clues to pick up the conversation when they are through.

Creative listening is showing a sincere interest in another person. You ask questions that will stimulate the conversation and get involved in their story. You can show your interest through statements that will encourage them to continue: "*That's fascinating*" or "*What happened next*". You can also keep the conversation going when there is a lull by a remark that ties in directly to that of the last person who spoke. "*Did I hear you mention you have been there, Lydia?*"

A creative listener feeds the current flow of conversation or adds new leads to the conversation by encouraging others to participate.

The Don'ts Of Conversation

Do not allow yourself or someone else to monopolize a conversation. If you sense this is happening, get someone else involved by adroitly changing the subject or asking someone else's opinion on the current subject. If you cannot successfully do this, excuse yourself from one group and move to another.

Do not try to impress people by using foreign languages or "drop in" phrases in French, Spanish, German, or any other language. The only time this is in good taste is when there is a guest that does not speak English.

And finally, make sure that no guest is left out of a conversation because they arrived "late" or the conversation is "over their head". If you want to become a good hostess or guest, it would be wise to try and find a subject that a person is able to talk intelligently about. You can discover this by talking to each individual and trying to expose their deepest interest and then channel a conversation in that direction. You may find that your part of the conversation will be phrases like, "*How exciting*!" or "*I never knew that!*", but the important thing is that your guest will consider you a wonderful conversationalist.

There should not be any attacks on anything, religion, political parties, races, etc. Reasonable discussions, yes, but *watch out*. Discussion in these areas can lead to heated exchanges. Your first duty as a hostess is to "protect" your guest. Your first duty as a guest is to "respect" the house you are visiting. You can best perform by eliminating strong statements on moral or ethnic topics. Eliminating or bypassing a conversation heading in this direction will suspend the possibility of someone being offended.

Once you have learned how to have a pleasant, attractive voice with proper speech, you can be a good conversationalists by remembering to be considerate of others. Remember that the same rules hold true in school environments, such as a meeting, or any time you are conversing with two or more people. If you practice the rules of being a good conversationalist, you will find you get more out of any conversation and learn more by just giving equal time to the participants.

This is what it takes to add the art of conversation and voice to your list of self-development training. You may want to stop at this point and review what you have learned. Go ahead, you have plenty of time. When you are ready, you'll go on to learn about poise and posture.

CONCLUSION

You are now half way through and there is still more important coverage to follow.

MASTERING GIRLHOOD TO WOMANHOOD, Book 4 introduces you to the following:

THE VISUALS: Good posture is seen to have many advantages. From an aesthetic point of view, it can enhance image, sending out the right signals (body language). But what is a good posture? We recognize poor posture when we see it, but just to confuse the matter, people with an ideal 'plumb-line' posture can also have poor movement patterns. This is because it is not the shape that is important but how it is maintained. An apparent 'good' posture can be achieved with inappropriate muscular activity. Posture is the manifestation of attitude and not simply a matter of muscle tone.

Poise is not acquired through conventional exercises that concentrate on the muscle. Poise comes with an understanding and experience of free movement and balance is vital for poise. Poise is a body state achieved only by steady and carefree education of the body and maintenance of balance.

THE ICING ON THE CAKE: Courtesy, politeness or having good manners are all about respecting others and yourself. Think about how you feel if someone: talked to your friend but turned his back to you, pushed you out of the way to get the seat you were about to sit on, or let the door slam in your face. Even never saying 'please' or 'thank you' is a deal or "friend" breaker.

Good manners are about considering the feelings of other people and being the kind of person that others will like and respect. If you show good manners everywhere you go, then you are more likely to encourage others to behave in the same way towards you.

speaking eloquently; proper etiquette is more than saying the proper, flowery things at the proper times.

YOU GO GIRL: If you are not prepared to handle outside pressures, you will after you have reviewed this lesson. You are introduced to feelings, peer pressure, self-esteem, bullying, and substance abuse. Knowing how to react and handle yourself is very important.

YOUR SEXUALITY: You are becoming a woman and as such you need to know not only what this means, but how you can prepare yourself to make the right decisions.

www.ingramcontent.com/pod-product-compliance
Lightning Source LLC
LaVergne TN
LVHW090937080826
845145LV00003B/780

* 9 7 8 1 9 2 8 6 1 3 4 7 3 *